AN INTRODUCTION
TO LABOR LAW

AN INTRODUCTION TO LABOR LAW

SECOND EDITION

Michael Evan Gold

ILR BULLETIN 66

ILR Press AN IMPRINT OF
Cornell University Press

ITHACA AND LONDON

Copyright © 1989, 1998 by Cornell University

All rights reserved. Except for brief quotations in a review, this book, or parts
thereof, must not be reproduced in any form without permission in writing
from the publisher. For information, address Cornell University Press,
Sage House, 512 East State Street, Ithaca, New York 14850.

First published 1989 by ILR Press
Second edition first published 1998 by ILR Press/Cornell Paperbacks

Printed in the United States of America

Library of Congress Cataloging-in-Publication Data

Gold, Michael Evan.
    An introduction to labor law / Michael Evan Gold.—2nd ed.
      p. cm. — (ILR bulletin ; 66)
Includes index.
    ISBN-13: 978-0-8014-8477-3 (pbk. : alk. paper)
    ISBN-10: 0-8014-8477-4 (pbk.)
    1. Labor law and legislation—United States. I. Title.
II. Series.
    KF3319.G62   1997
    344.7301—dc21
                                             97-30761

Cornell University Press strives to use environmentally responsible suppliers and
materials to the fullest extent possible in the publishing of its books. Such materials
include vegetable-based, low-VOC inks and acid-free papers that are recycled, totally
chlorine-free, or partly composed of nonwood fibers. For further information,
visit our website at www.cornellpress.cornell.edu.

5 7 9 Paperback printing 10 8 6

CONTENTS

PREFACE

The purpose of this bulletin is to introduce the reader to the federal law of unions and employers. This law is composed of two major elements. The first element is the statutes enacted by Congress: the National Labor Relations Act of 1935, the Labor-Management Relations Act of 1947, and later amendments. The second element is the decisions of the National Labor Relations Board and of the federal courts; these decisions interpret and apply the statutes.

The statutes are long and complex, and the decisions of the Labor Board and of the courts number in the hundreds of thousands. As a result, this bulletin cannot cover all of the law. Only the most important areas of the law are discussed, and the discussion of these areas is purposefully simplified. Although all of the following statements about the law are accurate, many are incomplete. Much more could be said about every topic addressed below.

Two types of reader are likely to benefit from reading this bulletin. One is the person who knows little or nothing about the law; the other is the person whose knowledge has become rusty with disuse. The former can learn, the latter can relearn, the basic principles and structures of the law. (These persons might also find useful another bulletin, *Industrial and Labor Relations Terms: A Glossary,* by Robert E. Doherty.)

One type of reader is unlikely to benefit from this bulletin: the person who needs to know whether specific conduct, arising in a context of many other facts, is legal or illegal. Too many rules have been omitted, too many qualifications have gone unstated, for this bulletin to serve this purpose. The reader who needs to know the law in a specific case should consult a comprehensive treatise on labor law or, better yet, a labor lawyer.

Peter Hoffman was kind enough to the author, and concerned enough about the reader, to study a draft of the second edition of this bulletin and suggest a number of improvements. Samuel Kaynard was equally generous with his time and intelligence for the first edition. Of course, any errors or misleading statements that occur are the responsibility of the author.

1

LABOR LAW BEFORE
THE LABOR ACT

MEANING OF "LABOR LAW"

The term "labor law" does not mean what it seems to. It seems to mean all of the law that applies to workers and employers. In fact, "labor law" refers to only a part of this law, namely, the law that applies to unions and private employers. The reason for the confusion is that, when the term "labor law" came into use, the major laws that existed regarding workers applied to unions and private employers. In the last sixty years, the law has grown to include topics such as minimum wages, health and safety on the job, unemployment insurance, pension plans, race and sex discrimination, and so forth. A new term, "employment law," has been coined for these laws. But "labor law" still means the law of unions and private employers, and this bulletin is about labor law.

EARLY LABOR LAW AS MADE BY THE COURTS

Most Americans believe that legislatures make the law and that courts apply the law to individual cases. As any lawyer will tell you, this belief is more false than true. It is somewhat true because legislatures do enact statutes, which the courts interpret and apply. But the belief is false because most law is actually made by the courts.

Courts make law in two ways. In the first way, which was more prevalent in the past, judges simply announced the law; we might say (though the judges never admitted it) that they invented the law. There existed few statutes passed by legislatures, and the judges used custom or applied their own ideas of right and wrong to cases. Such lawmaking is known as the "common law." The common law continues to affect our lives today, though less powerfully than in the past.

In the second way that courts make law, the starting point is a statute passed by a legislature. Now, if the case of *A v. B* falls squarely within the words of the statute, we may say that the legislature has made the law that governs that case. But what if the case of *C v. D* is just slightly outside the words of the statute? In this event, the judge must decide whether or not the statute applies to the case. In making this decision, the judge is making law for the parties to the case. Because of the doctrine of precedent, this new law will also control future cases that are similar to *C v. D*. Then the case of *E v. F* will come along, and it will be slightly different from any previous case; once again the judge will make new law in deciding this case. And then the case of *G v. H* will come up, and so on.

If a legislature is dissatisfied with a court's interpretation of a statute, the legislature has the power to amend the statute to override the court's interpretation; however, this power is not often exercised. As a result, most law is made by court decisions.

Employers took their labor troubles to court almost as soon as America became independent. We are a nation of many states; each state has its own courts, and they often have disagreed with one another about labor cases. As a result, accurate generalizations about labor law in the eighteenth and nineteenth centuries are hard to make. Nevertheless, most students of early labor law would probably agree that the courts in those days were unsympathetic to unions. Whenever unions devised an effective new tactic against employers, or found a way around existing laws, the courts responded to employers' complaints with new laws to control labor.

Because the First Amendment to the U.S. Constitution protects the freedom of association, the courts did not outlaw unions as such; but the courts did outlaw the tactics used by unions to improve their members' wages and working conditions. At the beginning of the nineteenth century, a common union tactic was for union members to agree among themselves how much in wages they would accept from their employers; the members also refused to work in the same shop as any other worker who accepted less than union scale. But the courts held that this tactic was a criminal conspiracy, and juries composed of shopkeepers and landowners convicted and fined union members for striking over wages.

By the end of the nineteenth century, prosecutions for criminal conspiracy had become ineffective in controlling labor unions. There were several reasons for this change. First, a criminal case was too slow. The workers could not be punished until after an indictment was issued and the case had gone to trial. This process often took several months, during which the strike or boycott was damaging the employer's business. Second, as the right to vote, which was once limited to property holders, was extended to all men (women did not get the right to vote until 1920), juries were increasingly made up of workers, not merely shopkeepers and landowners; and workers were hesitant to find coworkers guilty of the crime of peacefully trying to improve their wages and working conditions. Third, the law was changing so that in many places a strike was not considered an illegal conspiracy.

Employers, therefore, took their complaints to the civil courts, and here they found the perfect weapon for fighting unions: the injunction. An injunction is an order from a court requiring a person to do or not to do specific acts. A person can be sent to jail for violating an injunction. Injunctions are fast: one can be issued the very day it is requested. And injunctions are issued by judges, not juries. In the past, the law permitted judges to issue injunctions against unions freely. For example, the law authorizes an injunction to control violence and intimidation. Courts held that picket lines were "morally intimidating" and issued injunctions against picketing, even though the picketers merely walked back and forth and tried to talk workers and customers into going elsewhere.

ROLE OF ANTITRUST LAW

In 1890, Congress passed the Sherman Antitrust Act in order to control monopolies in business, but the wording of the law was so general that it could be applied to labor unions as well. The statute outlawed "every . . . combination . . . or conspiracy in restraint of trade or commerce among the several states." Although this act was not used against strikes over wages and hours, it was used to control union organizing. In the infamous *Danbury Hatters* case, the union sought to organize all the fur hat makers of America by boycotting the products of nonunion manufacturers. One manufacturer sued, arguing that the boycott was a "restraint of trade." The courts found that the boycott did diminish trade among the states and awarded hundreds of thousands of dollars of damages—payable by the individual workers! (The American Federation of Labor later raised the funds necessary to settle the case.)

Twenty-five years later, in 1914, Congress passed the Clayton Act, which stated, "the labor of a human being is not a commodity or article of commerce" and "no . . . injunction shall be granted in any case between an employer and employees . . . growing out of a dispute concerning terms or conditions of employment." Union leaders regarded the Clayton Act as a great victory for organized labor; Samuel Gompers, the first president of the American Federation of Labor, called the act "the Magna Carta of labor." But the courts turned the victory into defeat by holding that Congress did not mean to permit boycotts in support of organizing campaigns. Once again, employers, with willing aid from the courts, found a way to restrict the power of workers.

NORRIS-LAGUARDIA ACT

The modern law of labor relations begins with the Norris-LaGuardia Act of 1932, which is still in force today. With some exceptions, this statute restricts the power of federal courts to issue injunctions in cases growing out of labor disputes. One reason for this statute was that federal judges had created so much unfavorable law and issued so many crippling injunctions that the federal judiciary became, in the eyes of labor, the symbol as well as the instrument of anti-unionism. Another, perhaps more important reason for the statute was the Great Depression. Unemployment reached 25 percent or more, and today's social insurance programs (such as unemployment insurance and welfare) did not exist then. As a result, workers and their families suffered terribly. Organized labor spoke on their behalf. The Norris-LaGuardia Act was a step toward recognizing unions as the legitimate representatives of workers.

But Norris-LaGuardia was a small step, and it applied only to the federal courts. State courts were still free to issue injunctions in labor disputes (though some states later passed "little Norris-LaGuardia acts"). Also, both federal and state courts remained free to hold unions liable in civil suits, for example, for violation of antitrust laws. Perhaps most important, employers remained free to discharge workers who led, joined, or as much as sympathized with unions; and employers had no duty to bargain with unions, even if they represented a majority of workers. Further steps were necessary to empower labor unions.

2

AN INTRODUCTION TO
THE LABOR ACT

In 1935, Congress recognized unions as legitimate representatives of workers. The National Labor Relations Act (sometimes called the Wagner Act) required private employers to deal with unions and prohibited discrimination against union members. (Public employers—federal, state, and local governments—are not covered by the Labor Act.) Employers who violated the Labor Act could be tried before the National Labor Relations Board, which had the power to order them to stop the illegal behavior and compensate the victims for lost pay. As a check on the power of the Labor Board, the law provided that appeals from the Board's decisions could be taken to the federal appellate courts. The Courts were instructed to respect the Board's special expertise in labor affairs.

By 1947, unions had grown in power, and public opinion toward them turned hostile. Perhaps the greatest cause of this hostility was the wave of strikes after the Second World War. During the war, strikes were prohibited, and wages were controlled. Afterward, many unions struck to make up for what they had lost during the war. There was also a steep rise in inflation, which the public blamed on unions. In addition, management organized itself to fight the growing power of unions. The result was the Labor Management Relations Act (often called the Taft-Hartley Act). Its most important feature was that it outlawed certain practices by unions. Starting in 1947, the Labor Board and the courts had the power to order unions to stop unfair labor practices and to compensate the victims of that behavior.

Taft-Hartley was amended by the Labor-Management Reporting and Disclosure Act of 1959 (the Landrum-Griffin Act) and by the Health Care Amendments of 1974, but the basic structure of the law was not changed. In this bulletin, the term "Labor Act" will be used to refer to the law as it stands today. The main elements of that law are discussed below.

COVERAGE OF THE LABOR ACT

Most employees working for (or seeking jobs in) private firms are protected by the Labor Act. "Protected" means that the law shields employees against unfair labor practices and requires their employers to bargain with a union if it is chosen by a majority of the employees.

Some employees, however, are not protected by the Labor Act. The following classes of employees are not protected:

- employees of federal, state, or local governments;
- employees of railroads or airlines;
- agricultural workers;
- domestic servants working in their employer's home;
- spouses and children of employers;
- independent contractors;
- anyone who acts on behalf of the employer, for example, managers, supervisors, and confidential employees.

In some cases, employees who are not protected by the Labor Act are protected by other laws. For example, the Railway Labor Act covers employees of railroads and airlines; a few states have laws that apply to agricultural employees, and several states and the federal government protect governmental employees. Of course, such laws may differ from the Labor Act; therefore, the rules discussed in this bulletin may not apply to those workers.

Also, some classes of workers—for example, construction workers, health care workers, and guards—are covered by the Labor Act, but special rules apply to them. This bulletin does not include those special rules.

What happens if an employee who is protected by the Labor Act goes on strike? The Act specifically states that strikers remain employees, so strikers continue to enjoy the protection of the Act. But strikers lose their status as employees of the struck employer if they abandon the strike and take permanent jobs in other firms.*

EXCLUSIVITY OF REPRESENTATION

In the United States and Canada, the majority of workers in an appropriate bargaining unit decides whether or not all the workers in that unit

---

* The rights of strikers are discussed in chapters 4 and 6.

will be represented by a union. (An "appropriate bargaining unit" is a group of jobs that are similar in some ways.*) If a majority of workers in a bargaining unit chooses to be represented by a union, the employer must bargain with the union regarding *all* the workers, even those who would prefer to bargain individually with their employer. The union becomes the exclusive bargaining agent of the unit; the employer must bargain with this union and none other. But if the majority chooses *not* to be represented by a union, the employer need not bargain with the union, even though many workers might be members of it.

It is important to realize that *representation* by a union is separate from *membership* in a union. Membership is controlled by the union's own rules; the Labor Act says nothing about who may join a union. This fact affects representation in two ways that are illustrated by the following cases. First, Harry is the only person in his shop who is interested in joining a union. The union is free to accept Harry as a member. However, if the union tries to bargain on his behalf with his employer—for example, by trying to get a raise for Harry—the employer may ignore the union because it does not represent a majority of workers in the shop. Second, Mary wants to be a member of union A, but a majority of workers in the shop wants to be represented by union B. Mary is free to join union A, and it is free to accept her. However, the employer must bargain with union B regarding all workers, including Mary, because a majority has chosen union B. (Union security is discussed later in this chapter.[†] Here it should be noted that, if the employer and the union agree to a union shop or an agency shop, Mary could be required to pay dues to union B. But she need not join union B, and she may remain a member of union A.)

DUTY OF FAIR REPRESENTATION

From time to time, individual workers are likely to become unhappy with the union that represents them. Any organization run by majority rule has this problem; a minority can become dissatisfied. We normally are free to quit organizations that make us unhappy. But because of exclusivity of representation, a dissatisfied worker cannot escape representation by a union (unless one quits the job); as long as the majority wants

* For a fuller discussion appropriate bargaining units, see chapter 4, APPROPRIATE BARGAINING UNITS.
† See SECTION 8: UNFAIR LABOR PRACTICES, Union Security.

the union, it bargains for all workers, including those who are discontented.

Recognizing this problem, the law has created the duty of fair representation. As its name implies, this duty requires a union to represent each worker fairly; that is, the union must always have good reasons for what it does. The duty of fair representation applies both to negotiating contracts and to enforcing them.

Contract negotiations often force a union to make hard choices. For example, suppose skilled workers in a bargaining unit earn ten dollars an hour, and unskilled workers in the unit earn six dollars an hour. The union must decide the kind of pay increase to demand. On the one hand, if the union tries to get a 5 percent raise for everyone, the skilled workers will get a fifty-cent raise, while the unskilled workers will get only a thirty-cent raise. On the other hand, if the union tries to get fifty cents for everyone, the unskilled workers will get an 8 percent raise, but the skilled workers will get only 5 percent. Whichever choice the union makes, some workers will probably complain; yet it must make a choice. In such situations, the law permits the union a "wide range of reasonableness." Some workers win more than others in collective bargaining, and sometimes there are real losers. The union's choices are legal as long as they are made in good faith, that is, without an illegal purpose or a malicious intent to harm anyone. But if the union makes the decision based on bad reasons—for instance, decides that supporters of the winning candidate in the last union election will get big raises, while opponents will get laid off—the duty of fair representation would be violated.

Enforcing contracts also forces unions to make hard choices. The most common situation involves a grievance over discipline. Suppose, for example, that Mary is fired for insubordination. She files a grievance, but it cannot be settled. The question then becomes whether the union should take the case to arbitration. The grievance committee votes to drop the matter because the committee believes an arbitrator would deny the grievance. Mary, of course, is furious. Has the union represented her fairly? The law requires the union to investigate the grievance and make an impartial decision. Therefore, if the committee honestly believes the arbitration would be lost, the duty of fair representation would be satisfied. But if the committee's real reason is illegitimate, the duty of fair representation would be violated. For example, the duty would be violated if the committee refused to process Mary's grievance because members of the committee dislike Mary as a person. Race and sex discrimination by a union also breach the duty of fair representation. It would be illegal to drop Mary's grievance because she is a woman or because of her race.

The duty of fair representation covers all workers who are represented by a union. The duty applies whether or not the worker is a member of the union.

A worker who believes the duty of fair representation has been violated can pursue either of two remedies. One remedy is to file a lawsuit against the union. If the employer is involved in the case, the worker may also sue the employer. Thus, in Mary's case, she believes that the employer violated the contract by firing her without just cause and that the union breached the duty of fair representation by refusing to arbitrate the matter; so she would sue them both in court. The other remedy is for the worker to file a charge of unfair labor practice against the union with the Labor Board. A charge could not be filed against the employer in a case like this, however.

Which is the better remedy for the worker? There are two considerations. First, the worker who goes to the Labor Board incurs no cost because the government pays for the investigation and trial, whereas the worker who hires an attorney to file a private lawsuit might incur substantial costs. Second, the Labor Board usually will not act against an employer in a fair representation case. Therefore, if only the union is at fault, a charge filed with the Board might be sufficient; but if the employer is also at fault, only a lawsuit could provide complete relief.

SECTION 7: PROTECTION FOR CONCERTED ACTIVITY

The heart of the Labor Act is its section 7. The central idea of section 7 is to give workers the legal right to negotiate with their employer as a group instead of as individuals. Congress created this right because individuals have little bargaining power when they deal with employers, particularly large corporations. The result of this lack of power is that workers can be forced to accept low wages and poor working conditions. But if workers can band together and, as a group—usually, through a union—negotiate with their employer, they have a better chance to achieve a living wage and decent conditions of work.

To reach these goals, section 7 guarantees employees the right to engage in concerted activity, which means the right to act together to improve their working lives. The right to concerted activity includes the rights to assist and to join labor unions. Employers are forbidden to interfere with these activities. For example, it would be an unfair labor practice for an employer to fire a worker for going to the union hall to hear a speech.

Congress recognized that some workers prefer not to engage in concerted activity. Therefore, section 7 also guarantees employees the right to refrain from assisting and joining unions. Unions and employers are forbidden to interfere with this right as well. (An exception to this right is the union security clause, which is discussed later in this chapter.*) For example, it would be an unfair labor practice for a union to threaten to use violence against a worker who refused to join the union, or to discriminate against a worker who refused to support the union in a representation election.

The protection of concerted activity in section 7 includes workers on the job. In one case, an employer called a worker into the office and accused her of stealing. She asked to have her shop steward present during the rest of the interview; the employer refused. The Supreme Court held that a worker who reasonably believes an interview will lead to discipline has a right to have a union representative present. (The Court also held that the employer may choose to cancel the interview and investigate the matter without hearing from the worker, rather than let the union representative attend the interview.) The Labor Board has ruled that a worker has no right to have a union steward present if the purpose of the interview is merely to inform the worker of discipline that the employer has already decided upon. The Board has also ruled that a worker in a non-union shop does not have a right to a representative.

A question that is still unresolved is whether section 7 protects sympathy strikers, for example, workers who refuse to cross a picket line at another employer's place of business. Some courts hold that sympathy strikers are not engaged in concerted activity because they have nothing in common with the workers of the other employer; therefore, the employer may fire the sympathy strikers. Other courts hold that workers are entitled to make common cause with any other workers; therefore, sympathy strikers may not be fired because honoring a picket line is like going on strike. But even these latter courts limit the workers' protection in two ways. First, workers who refuse to cross a picket line have the same

* SECTION 8: UNFAIR LABOR PRACTICES, Union Security.

status as the picketers. Thus, if the picketers are on an illegal strike, a worker who honored the picket line could be fired. If the picketers are on a lawful economic strike, a worker who honored the picket line could be permanently replaced.* Second, if sympathy strikers are covered by a labor contract that specifically gives up the right of workers to engage in a sympathy strike, the employer may fire them for violating the contract. What if the contract generally gives up the right to strike—but does not specifically mention sympathy strikes? Many contracts contain broad no-strike clauses (in which the union promises not to strike during the term of the contract for any reason) but do not specifically refer to sympathy strikes. A conservative Board created a presumption that broad no-strike clauses prohibit sympathy strikes; that is, sympathy strikes are illegal unless other evidence shows the parties specifically intended to permit them. A liberal Board reversed that presumption, holding that broad no-strike clauses allow sympathy strikes unless the evidence shows the parties specifically intended to prohibit them.

Even workers who are engaged in concerted activity can get themselves in trouble if they go too far. Suppose the union is on strike over wages, and Mary is walking the picket line in front of the shop. Striking is concerted activity, and the employer may not punish Mary for it. Now suppose a customer tries to enter the shop, and Mary blocks the door; or suppose a delivery truck pulls up, and Mary puts tacks under the tires. In cases like these, workers are no longer protected by the Labor Act. They have engaged in misconduct, and the employer is free to fire them.

Section 7 also guarantees the right of employees to engage in collective bargaining through the union of their choice. This right would be violated, for example, if an employer tried to force workers to join union A instead of union B.

SECTION 8: UNFAIR LABOR PRACTICES

Up to this point, a few specific unfair labor practices have been mentioned, but the general categories of unfair labor practices have not been described. These categories are contained in section 8(a), which pertains to employers, and section 8(b), which pertains to unions.

---

* The rights of economic strikers and the difference between being fired and being permanently replaced are discussed in chapter 4.

Before we discuss the categories, a word about responsibility is in order. An agent is someone who acts on behalf of someone else. Employers and unions are responsible for the acts of their agents. This rule holds whether or not the employer or union is unaware of the agent's illegal conduct; the rule holds even if the employer or union has a policy prohibiting the illegal conduct. Thus, if a foreman fires a worker because she favors the union, the employer cannot escape responsibility by arguing that he did not know what the foreman was doing; the company has committed an unfair labor practice. If a business agent of a union threatens to pulverize a worker if he does not join at once, the union cannot escape responsibility by arguing that the union has a policy against intimidation; the union has committed an unfair labor practice.

Interference with Concerted Activity

Section 8(a)(1) prohibits an employer from interfering with employees as they engage in concerted activity. At the same time, the right of the employer to operate an efficient business must be respected. The employer's right is important because many actions taken by an employer interfere with concerted activity to some extent, yet they are justified by genuine needs of the business. In general, therefore, the right of workers to be free from interference with concerted activity must be balanced against the right of the employer to run the business. For example, suppose a firm normally closes at 5:00 P.M. and its workers decide to hold a meeting at 5:30 on Tuesday to discuss whether to form a union. On Monday the firm receives a rush order that requires the workers to put in overtime for the entire week. Although the overtime interferes with the workers' right to form a labor union, the interference would not be an unfair labor practice. Nonetheless, if the employer scheduled overtime purposely to prevent the workers from holding their meeting, there would be no legitimate business interest to balance against the interference, and, as a result, section 8(a)(1) would be violated.

Section 8(b)(1) prohibits a union from restraining or coercing employees as they exercise their section 7 rights. For example, section 7 protects the right of employees to refrain from concerted activity. Being a member of a union is a form of concerted activity. It follows that a union may not prohibit its members from resigning from the union, that is, from ceasing concerted activity. This rule applies at all times, even during a strike; accordingly, a union may not discipline a worker who resigns from the

union during a strike and goes back to work. Section 8(b)(1) also prohibits a union from coercing an employer in the selection of representatives for collective bargaining.

Dominating or Assisting a Labor Union

Section 8(a)(2) prohibits an employer from dominating or assisting a
labor union. The union must be independent and free of the employer's
influence, whether that influence is harmful or helpful. Accordingly, an
employer may not provide financial support to a union, for example,
excessive free use of the employer's secretarial staff; however, a mod-
est amount of support, such as posting union notices on company bulletin boards or using a room in the company building for a union meeting, is permissible. (Note that a labor contract may require an employer
to collect union dues from workers and turn them over to the union; this
is called a "checkoff," and it is legal as long as the workers authorize
it.)

Recent innovations in personnel management, such as "employee involvement programs," have raised questions under section 8(a)(2).
Whereas our national labor policy encourages cooperation and communi-
cation between workers and managers, that same policy outlaws sham
unions, which fool workers into believing that they are getting the benefit of collective bargaining without a union. In a recent case, an employer
created "action committees" to cope with employee dissatisfaction over a
number of issues such as pay, attendance, and smoking rules. The employer decided which workers would serve on the committees, appointed
representatives of management to the committees, and specified the procedures and goals of the committees. Management reserved the right to
accept or reject any proposals made by the committees. The Board held
that these committees violated section 8(a)(2) because, although it ap-
peared to workers that they and management were jointly exercising the
power to resolve their disagreements, in fact the employer reserved all
power to itself.

As the law now stands, an employer may create joint worker-manage-
ment committees for the purposes of improving efficiency or communi-
cation, for example, a committee to plan the way work will be done or to
pass information back and forth. An employer may not, however, deal
with or bargain with such committees over the terms and conditions of
employment.

Discrimination Because of Concerted Activity

Section 8(a)(3) makes it an unfair labor practice for an employer to discriminate against any worker because he has engaged in, or refrained from, union activity. Section 8(b)(2) makes it illegal for a union to cause (or attempt to cause) an employer to discriminate in violation of section 8(a)(3)

Discrimination has two elements: a harmful act and an improper motive for the act. As a rule, unless both elements are present, the employer's act is lawful. Thus, many acts by an employer are harmful to a worker—layoff, denial of overtime, and discharge, to name a few. Yet these acts are not illegal unless the motive behind them is improper. It is not an unfair labor practice to lay off a worker because business is bad, but it is illegal to lay off a worker because he has been agitating for the union. Similarly, it is not an unfair labor practice for a union to insist that Harry be laid off instead of Mary because she has more seniority, but it would be illegal for the union to do so because Harry refused to join the union.

Union Security

Sections 8(a)(3) and 8(b)(2) also regulate union security clauses, which are sections of collective bargaining agreements that deal with the workers' relationship to the union. There are different kinds of union security clauses. In a closed shop, the employer agrees to hire only persons who are already members of the union; the employer also agrees to fire anyone whom the union expels from membership. The Labor Act outlaws the closed shop.

In the agency shop, the employer may hire a worker who is not a member of the union; but within thirty days the worker must pay the union an initiation fee, and the worker must pay regular union dues thereafter. Agency shops are lawful. The worker is not required to join the union, but he is required to pay the union for the services it provides. If the worker fails to pay the money, the union may insist that the employer fire him.

In the union shop, an employer may hire a worker who is not a member of the union, but the worker must join the union within thirty days or be fired. (Somewhat different rules apply in the construction industry.) The Labor Act is ambiguous about the legality of the union shop. The first proviso to section 8(a)(3) states that a labor agreement may require a worker to become a member of a union within thirty days of being hired. But the second proviso to the same section states that an employer may fire an employee whom the union excludes from membership, or whom the union expels, only if the exclusion or expulsion occurred because the employee did not pay the union's regular initiation fee and dues. Thus, the first proviso seems to authorize a union shop, while the second proviso seems to outlaw the union shop and permit only an agency shop. The Supreme Court has held that the second proviso is controlling. Therefore, the law does not permit an employer and a union to coerce a worker into joining the union. Nevertheless, union shop clauses are common in labor contracts. Because of the law, a union and an employer usually treat a union shop clause as though it created an agency shop; if the worker pays the initiation fee and dues, but refuses to join, he is permitted to keep his job.

The difference between a union shop and an agency shop is that the worker must join the union in a union shop, but need only pay initiation fees and dues in an agency shop. The difference between joining and paying dues is important. A worker who merely pays dues does not become a member and may ignore the union's rules. A worker who joins a union becomes a member and must obey its rules. If he breaks a rule, he can be disciplined, for example, by a fine. (However, even if he breaks twenty rules, the union may not discipline him by forcing the employer to fire him. Also, as noted above, a member may resign from a union at any time. If he joined because the contract contained a union shop clause and he did not know that he only had to pay dues, he is free to quit; but he must continue to pay dues.)

Because of religious beliefs, some workers refuse to join a union or pay money to one. Without special accommodations, such workers could not hold a job in a union shop or an agency shop. Section 19 of the Labor Act accommodates to such beliefs by providing that a union security clause may not be applied to religious objectors. However, to alleviate the problem of the "free rider"—that is, a person who enjoys the benefits of union representation without paying for those benefits—a religious objector may be required to pay the equivalent of initiation fees and dues to a nonreligious charity. One court has held that Section 19 is unconstitutional.

In an open shop, a union represents a bargaining unit, but no worker is required to join the union or pay dues. Section 14(b) of the Labor Act allows individual states to pass laws prohibiting union security clauses— that is, requiring the open shop within their borders. These laws are known as "right-to-work" laws, and about twenty states have them. (The specific content of right-to-work laws varies in different states.) Even though a right-to-work law may exist in a state, a union operating in that state is still bound by the duty of fair representation. That is, the union must represent each worker in a bargaining unit, whether or not the worker is a member of the union.

An issue that the courts have dealt with for many years is how a union may spend dues money. Suppose the majority of members of a union authorizes it to spend dues for a certain purpose, but a dues payer objects. (This person might be a member who has voluntarily joined the union, or a nonmember who pays dues because of a union security clause.) Is the objecting worker entitled to a partial refund? The answer depends on the purpose. At one extreme, it has always been clear that a union may spend dues for purposes of collective bargaining. This is the very reason that the union exists; if individual workers could object to using their money for collective bargaining, union security clauses would be meaningless. At the other extreme, a union may not spend a dues payer's money for political purposes, for example, lobbying Congress to change the law in a way favorable to unions, if the worker objects. The right of free speech means that no one should be compelled to spend money in support of political activity to which one objects. Drawing the line between these extremes is not easy. In general, the rule is that a union has the right to spend dues only for collective bargaining; a worker may object to, and receive a refund for, dues spent for any other purpose. But this rule raises the issue, what is collective bargaining? The answer can only be given in specific cases. The courts have held that negotiating a contract is part of collective bargaining, as is adjusting a grievance; but organizing new shops is not collective bargaining, nor are contributions to charitable causes. (Note that the Labor Act does not prohibit a union from spending dues for purposes other than collective bargaining. The Act merely entitles an objecting dues payer to a refund of dues used for such purposes.)

Retaliation

Section 8(a)(4) prohibits an employer from punishing a worker for filing charges with the Labor Board. The section also protects workers who testify in a hearing before the Board or give sworn statements to investigators from the Board.

Bargaining in Good Faith

If workers choose a union to represent them, sections 8(a)(5) and 8(b)(3) require the employer and the union to bargain collectively with each other in good faith. Collective bargaining means meetings between an employer and a union to discuss the creation or renewal of a labor contract, or to discuss a grievance, that is, a disagreement over how an existing labor contract should be applied in a particular situation. The duty to bargain is the legal requirement that an employer and a union meet at reasonable times and negotiate over important issues, such as wages, hours, and other conditions of employment. The parties must sincerely attempt to reach an agreement, but the Labor Act recognizes that agreement is not always possible; accordingly, the law specifically states that neither party is required to agree to a proposal or to make a concession.*

Remedies for Unfair Labor Practices

If an employer or a union commits an unfair labor practice, the Board must order the guilty party to cease and desist from the illegal behavior—in other words, to stop it at once and never do it again. Also, unfair labor practices often cause injury to individuals. For example, if a worker is fired because she supported the union, she loses her job, her wages and benefits, and her seniority. To make up for these losses, the Board may order the employer to reinstate (rehire) her, pay her the wages and benefits she lost, and credit her with seniority as though she had never left work. This worker could suffer other losses as well. Without regular wages, she might be unable to make the payments on her car, and it might be repossessed; or if she borrowed money to make the payments, she would have to pay interest on the loan. Nevertheless, the Board will not order the employer to pay for losses like these. Also, the law requires the worker to make reasonable efforts to find other work; if the employer proves that she did not seek work during a calendar quarter, she will receive no back pay for that quarter.

The Labor Board routinely orders parties who are guilty of unfair labor practices to post a notice informing workers of the Board's decision. The notice states the behavior that the guilty party must not repeat and the action that the party must take to remedy the illegal behavior.

---

* The duty to bargain is discussed in more detail in chapter 5.

3

THE LABOR BOARD

The National Labor Relations Board (NLRB) has primary responsibility for administering the Labor Act. The Board is located in Washington, D.C., and has two branches. One branch is the Board itself. It has five members, though most cases are decided by panels of three members. The other branch is the Office of the General Counsel. The General Counsel is an independent officer who is responsible for prosecuting unfair labor practice cases.

The Board has divided the country into a number of regions, each of which has an office. The regional office is composed of a regional director and a staff of agents and attorneys. Any matter pertaining to the Labor Act must be brought first to the appropriate regional office; thus, if a worker believes that her employer committed an unfair labor practice in Ithaca, New York, she should contact the Board's regional office in Buffalo. If she does not know where the regional office is, she could call the Board in Washington, D.C., and ask for help. Appeals from decisions made in a regional office may be taken to the Board or the General Counsel in Washington.

UNFAIR LABOR PRACTICE CASES

The Labor Board deals with two kinds of cases. The first involves unfair labor practices, which will be discussed in the following paragraphs. The second involves representation of workers, which will be discussed later in this chapter.*

The issue in an unfair labor practice case is whether an employer or a

---

* See REPRESENTATION CASES.

union has violated the Labor Act. Such a case begins with a charge filed in the appropriate regional office of the Board. Anyone may file a charge. Naturally, the victim of the unfair labor practice may file a charge; a friend of the victim may file a charge or, as often happens, a union may file a charge in behalf of the victim. Similarly, employers, workers, and friends may file charges against unions. Members and agents of the Board do not file charges.

The statute of limitations in unfair labor practice cases is short. A charge must be filed within six months of the illegal act.

After a charge is filed, it is assigned to an agent in the regional office for investigation. The first question the agent asks is, Does the charge raise a violation of the Labor Act? If not, the charge must be dismissed. For example, suppose a charge alleged that the employer fired Harry because of his race. Because the Equal Employment Opportunity Commission, not the Labor Board, is responsible for charges of racial discrimination, the regional director would have to dismiss such a charge.

If the charge does state a violation of the Labor Act, the agent investigates to find out if there is reasonable cause to believe the allegations are true. Suppose, for example, a union files a charge alleging that an employer fired a worker because he was trying to persuade coworkers to vote for the union. Persuasion of this sort is concerted activity, and firing a worker for such persuasion is discrimination; therefore, the charge alleges a violation of section 8(a)(3) of the Labor Act, and the agent's task is to find out if the facts alleged in the charge are true. Usually, the agent interviews the charging party (the person who filed the charge) and his witnesses, as well as the respondent (the person accused of committing the unfair labor practice) and her witnesses. The agent commonly writes out a statement containing the evidence a witness has supplied and asks the witness to swear the statement is true. To protect witnesses, the Board keeps these statements confidential; however, a witness may ask for a copy of the statement (and may give it to the union or the employer). If the evidence supports the charge, the case will proceed to the next step. If the evidence does not support the charge, the regional director will dismiss it. Dismissal would be appropriate in the example above if the regional director believed the worker was fired for poor job performance, not for persuading coworkers to vote for the union.

Thus, the regional director will dismiss a charge if it does not allege a violation of the law, or if the charge alleges a violation, but the evidence does not support it. In either case, the charging party may appeal the dismissal to the General Counsel in Washington. If the General Counsel agrees with the regional director, the case is closed; there is no appeal to the courts on such dismissal of a charge. But if the General Counsel overrules the regional director (or, of course, if the evidence supports the charge), the case goes forward.

The next step is settlement. If the evidence supports the charge, the agent will try to settle the case. Returning to the example above, suppose the agent concludes that the worker was fired because he tried to persuade coworkers to vote for the union. In this event, the agent will urge the employer to agree to stop discriminating against workers because of their concerted activity; to reinstate the worker with back pay, benefits, and seniority; and to post a notice of the settlement in the shop for all the workers to see. Many cases are settled in this manner.

If settlement is not achieved, the regional director will issue a formal complaint against the respondent. The complaint is a legal document, similar to the complaints filed in the courts, and the respondent routinely hires an attorney to handle the case. Attempts at settlement continue; indeed, most cases are settled before they go to trial. But if settlement fails, there will be a trial before a federal administrative law judge (ALJ). The trial may be held in the regional office of the Board or at a place near the employer's business. Trials of unfair labor practice complaints are similar to trials in federal courts. The Labor Board's attorney prosecutes the case, and the respondent's attorney presents the defense. But two ways may be noted in which trials of unfair labor practices differ from court trials. First, there are no juries; the administrative law judge rules on the facts and the law. Second, the charging party may appear himself or send a representative (often an attorney) to participate in the trial. In our example, if settlement fails, the Board's attorney will present evidence that the worker was fired because he tried to persuade coworkers to vote for the union. The union's attorney may offer further evidence to the same effect. Then the employer's attorney will try to prove that the worker was really fired because of poor performance on the job.

Settlement efforts will continue even after the trial. If they fail again, the judge will decide the case. The charging party, the respondent, or the General Counsel may appeal this decision to the Labor Board in Washington. The Board may adopt the decision of the administrative law judge or modify or reverse it.

Appeals

If the Board rules in favor of the General Counsel (finds the respondent committed an unfair labor practice), it will issue a remedial order. The respondent has a legal duty to obey the Board's order; however, the Board cannot compel the respondent to obey. If the respondent does not voluntarily obey the order, the General Counsel must petition a federal Court of Appeals to order the respondent to obey. The respondent may argue to the court that the order should not be enforced because the Board's decision is erroneous. In this way, a respondent may secure judicial review of a decision by the Board.

A charging party may also secure judicial review of a decision by the Board. If the Board rules in favor of the respondent (finds the respondent did not commit an unfair labor practice), the charging party may appeal to a federal Court of Appeals, asking the court to reverse the Board's decision. (Being an agent of the Board, the General Counsel, of course, may not ask the court to overrule the Board.)

The loser in the Court of Appeals may ask the Supreme Court to review the case, but the high court accepts only a few such cases.

REPRESENTATION CASES

The discussion so far has focused on unfair labor practice cases, in which the issue is whether an employer or a union violated the Labor Act. The discussion will now shift to representation cases, in which the issue is whether a union is entitled to represent a unit of workers.

Three kinds of representation cases will be considered here: those involving certification of a union, those involving decertification of a union, and those involving unions that are competing with one another. In certification cases, the issue is whether a union should become the bargaining agent for a unit of workers. In decertification cases, the issue is whether a union should continue to be the bargaining agent for workers whom the union presently represents. In rival union cases, the issue is which of two or more unions should represent a unit of workers.

Certification Cases

Sometimes an employer directly recognizes a union; that is, the employer and the union agree that a majority of workers in an appropriate bargaining unit wants the union to represent them. After direct recognition, collective bargaining begins. Suppose, for example, that most of the workers in a small shop decide they want a union, and they join it. Then the union informs the employer of what has happened and asks to set a date to begin collective bargaining. The employer may know that the majority wants the union. Also, the employer may agree that the jobs make up an appropriate bargaining unit.* In this event, the employer may directly recognize the union and begin to bargain.

Usually, however, an employer will not directly recognize a union. She may doubt that most workers want a union, or she may want a chance to persuade them to change their minds. Or, as often happens, the employer may not agree that the jobs identified by the union make up an appropriate bargaining unit. The Labor Act provides a way of dealing with such cases.

The usual certification case begins when a worker approaches a union and says that conditions are not good in the shop. The union will encourage the worker to join the union and to recruit coworkers to join as well; sometimes the union will assign a paid organizer to assist in the recruiting. When 30 percent of the workers in a bargaining unit have joined the union, or authorized it to represent them, it may file a petition with the regional office of the Labor Board that is responsible for the shop. (As a rule, the union will not file a petition until a strong majority wants the union, but 30 percent is all the Board requires.) The petition describes the unit that the union wants to represent and asks the Board to hold an election.

The employer may object to the petition. One common objection is that the unit is not appropriate, that is, the jobs in the unit are so different that collective bargaining for the workers who hold these jobs would be unusually difficult. The regional director will decide whether the unit requested by the union is appropriate. This decision must be made before the election is held because only workers who hold jobs in the unit will be allowed to vote. (To protect against the possibility that the Board will agree with the employer that the unit is not appropriate, the union's petition often asks to represent "this unit or any other appropriate unit"; if the union does not get its first choice of units, it may be satisfied with its second choice.)

Another issue that may arise before an election is which workers are

---

* Appropriate bargaining units are discussed in chapter 4, APPROPRIATE BARGAINING UNITS.

eligible to vote. Some workers may be on layoff, others on sick leave, and there may be regular part-time and seasonal workers. The Board has specific regulations regarding these questions; they are mentioned in chapter 4.* What matters now is that a union and an employer can disagree about who is eligible to vote in an election, and the regional director must make a decision.

Before deciding on issues like these, the regional director normally assigns an agent of the Board to investigate. Also, a vigorous effort is made to encourage the parties to settle the issues. If settlement is not reached, often a hearing is held at which the union and the employer can offer evidence. After the hearing, the regional director issues a decision.

If the regional director's decision finds the unit requested by the union (or another unit acceptable to the union) is appropriate, the Board will conduct an election. Typically, a notice will be posted in the shop, stating when and where the election will be held. An agent of the Board will bring the ballot box and supervise the voting, which is done by secret ballot as in a public election. Representatives of the employer and of the union may observe. When balloting is completed, the agent will count the votes and announce the results.

Either party may raise objections to the election. One issue might be how to count a ballot that was marked improperly. Suppose, for example, a voter did not check one of the boxes, but instead wrote, "I hate unions." Another issue might be whether the person who voted was the authorized voter or an impostor. A third issue might be whether one party's conduct before the election wrongfully influenced the workers (for example, via bribes or threats), necessitating a new election. If such issues arise, the regional office will investigate them, and perhaps hold a hearing, after which the regional director will issue a decision.

Decertification Cases

The issue in decertification cases is whether a union should cease being the bargaining agent of a unit that the union already represents.

Occasionally, a union abandons a unit, that is, the union goes out of business or decides it no longer wishes to represent a group of workers. For example, if all the workers in a shop become unhappy with their union, the union might decide it cannot satisfy the workers, and walk

---

* See chapter 4, ELECTIONS, Eligibility to Vote in General.

away from them. In this event, the employer and the workers return to individual bargaining.

More commonly, some workers become unhappy, but the union believes that it is doing a good job, or can improve, and that it still represents the majority. If at least 30 percent of the workers in the unit show an interest in getting rid of the union, they may file a petition for decertification with the regional office of the Board, and an election will be held. The ballot will allow the workers to choose between being represented by the union or having no union.

Many of the issues that arise in decertification cases are the same as those that arise in certification cases. Issues in decertification cases may concern misconduct before the election, mismarked ballots, and eligible voters. The regional director will decide such issues in the same way as in certification cases.

Rival Unions

Sometimes two or more unions compete to represent a unit of workers. Such competition can occur either before any union represents the workers or after a union has represented the workers for a period of time.

Suppose a unit of workers is not represented by a union. Some of the workers approach union A and begin an organizing drive. Other workers approach union B and also begin a drive. Union A obtains authorization cards from 30 percent of the workers in the unit. Union B also obtains authorization cards from a substantial number of workers. In this case, the Board will hold an election in which the voters have three choices: union A, union B, or no union.

Now suppose a unit of workers is already represented by union A, but many workers are dissatisfied with the union. Workers have a right to change unions. If 30 percent of the unit signs a petition, the Board will hold an election in which the voters may choose between the rival unions.

Appeals

Decisions of the regional director in representation cases may be appealed to the Labor Board in Washington. But unlike unfair labor practice cases, there is no appeal in representation cases to the courts. The decision of the Board in a representation case is supposed to be final.

In fact, however, the Labor Board's decision in a representation case is not final. An indirect and time-consuming route is open to an employer. If the Board's decision goes against him, he may refuse to bargain with the union. The union will charge him with an unfair labor practice. He will defend on the ground that the bargaining unit is not appropriate, or ineligible persons were allowed to vote, and so on. The Board, having already rejected these arguments, will find the employer guilty. But, as noted above, an employer has no obligation to obey an order of the Board. Therefore, he can ignore the Board's decision and wait until the Board applies for a court order. In the judicial proceeding, the employer will present his arguments (the bargaining unit is inappropriate, and so on) and, if the court accepts them, it will refuse to enforce the Board's order. Of course, if the court rejects the employer's arguments, it will order him to comply with the Board's decision. This process consumes at least one year, and often two; and, during this time, the employer is not bargaining with the union. Regardless of whether he wins or loses, unless the employer commits an unfair labor practice (such as a unilateral change), he will pay no price for having refused to bargain while the case was in court.

4

ORGANIZING AND
ELECTIONS

As noted in chapter 3, an employer may extend direct recognition to a union that represents the majority of workers in a bargaining unit.* In this event, the law is not actively involved in the creation of the bargaining relationship. But, as was also noted, disputes can arise between the employer and the union, and the law becomes involved in settling those disputes. Important issues may arise, including: Which jobs should be grouped together into a bargaining unit? How should unions and employers conduct themselves during pre-election campaigns? Who should vote in the election? This chapter presents the law's answers to these questions.

APPROPRIATE BARGAINING UNITS

The idea behind an appropriate bargaining unit is to promote stability in the union-employer relationship, that is, to promote negotiated settlements instead of industrial warfare. If dissimilar jobs were joined in the same bargaining unit, the workers would have different needs and might be unable to agree on common goals. Division within the union might make collective bargaining difficult, perhaps leading to strikes and lockouts. In contrast, if the jobs in a unit are similar, the workers probably have similar needs and desires. Collective bargaining will be simpler because the range of issues will be limited, and negotiated settlements will become more likely.

If the employer and the union cannot agree on the bargaining unit, the Labor Board will make the decision. It was mentioned in chapter 3 that the petition for an election describes the unit that the union wants to rep-

* See chapter 3, REPRESENTATION CASES, Certification Cases.

resent. In deciding whether this (or any other) unit is appropriate, the Board's overriding concern is whether there is a community of interest. The Board asks, Do these jobs have enough in common that bargaining for them as a group is likely to be successful? The elements of community of interest include

- commonality of supervision;
- shared working areas;
- similarity of job duties;
- interchange of duties among jobs;
- employee transfers;
- similarity of methods of evaluating job performance;
- similarity of methods and rates of pay and other benefits;
- integration (that is, interdependence) of operations;
- history (if any) of collective bargaining between the parties.

Two points about these elements or criteria are worth noting. First, they apply to jobs, not workers. It does not matter whether Harry and Mary are bitter personal enemies; if their jobs are similar, they may be put in the same unit. And if Harry and Mary perform different tasks, have different supervisors, are paid by different methods, and work in different areas, their jobs will probably be put in different units, even if they are the best of friends. Second, it is common that a set of jobs could be grouped in two or more appropriate units. For example, a department store employs sales clerks, stock clerks, and warehouse workers. Each job could be a separate unit; but the stock clerks might fit well into a unit with either warehouse workers or sales clerks, and perhaps all three jobs could be combined into a single unit. In cases like this, the union is generally free to choose any appropriate unit. The Labor Board's job is not to find the *most* appropriate unit, but rather to decide whether the union has requested *an* appropriate unit.

Multi-plant and Multi-employer Units

Bargaining units are usually made up of some or all of the workers in a single shop or plant, for example, the carpenters on a construction project or all the workers in a paper mill. Sometimes, however, a bargaining unit will cover more than one facility. If a bargaining unit includes two or more plants, all of which are owned by the same employer, it is known as a multi-plant unit. If a bargaining unit includes two or more plants that are owned by different employers, it is known as a multi-employer unit.

A multi-plant unit (several plants, one employer) can be created in two ways. The union and the employer may agree to it, or the Labor Board can order its creation. Although it begins with a presumption in favor of a single-plant unit, the Board may create a multi-plant unit if the following conditions are present:

- centralization of management (particularly labor policy);
- short distance between the plants;
- significant interchange of employees among the plants.

A frequent example is a unit composed of several retail stores that are part of the same chain in the same area. Personnel policy often flows from a central office; the stores are within commuting distance of one another, and employees commonly move from one store to another.

A multi-employer unit (several plants, different employers) can be created only by agreement of the parties. The Board will never order separate employers to bargain jointly. The agreement to create a multi-employer unit is usually in writing, but it does not have to be; if separate employers bargain jointly over a period of time, the Board may find they have created a multi-employer unit. Once such a unit has been created, an employer or a union may withdraw from it by giving written notice to the other parties. Withdrawal is permitted prior to negotiations; however, once negotiations have begun, withdrawal is prohibited (except under extraordinary circumstances or by agreement of the parties).

ORGANIZING

Organizing begins as soon as one worker talks to another about improving their pay or working conditions. If enough workers want change, a union may launch an organizing campaign. A number of legal issues can arise during organizing. The rules that follow are the same for one worker talking to another and for a large-scale union campaign.

Solicitation on Company Property

One issue is whether employees may engage in concerted activity, for example, solicit one another to join the union, while they are on company property. Of course, work time is for work, and an employer may prohibit solicitation on company property during working time. But during non-working time—for example, lunch time, rest breaks, and before and after shifts—it is an unfair labor practice for an employer to interfere with union solicitation. (The right of employees to engage in concerted activity on company property during nonworking time has been extended. The right applies after the union has become the bargaining agent and the workers want to conduct union business, such as discussing a grievance. The right also protects workers who want to criticize their union.)

What if a union organizer, who is not an employee of a firm, wants to enter the firm's property to solicit for the union? The law allows the employer to exclude the organizer, both during working time and during nonworking time (except in the unusual case in which the union has no alternative way to reach the workers). This rule, which is based on the employer's property rights, makes it difficult for a union to bring its message to workers. But the Labor Board requires an employer, soon after the regional director decides it is appropriate to hold an election, to give the regional director a list of the names and addresses of eligible voters; and the regional director then turns this list over to the union. Having this list somewhat eases the union's difficulty in contacting workers.

Use of Propaganda

How the law should treat campaign propaganda is a controversial question. Both sides enjoy the right to free speech, but does free speech include stretching the truth? Should a new election be held if the winner has lied to the workers? Over the years, the Board has said both yes and no. When the answer is no, the argument is that a union election is like a political election: workers are adults who know propaganda when they see it. Also, the other party will probably discover the lie and use it against the liar. When the answer is yes, the argument is that a union election is very different from a political election: employers and unions have great power over workers, whereas candidates for public office go begging for votes; because of the power of employers and unions, workers may not realize they are being lied to. Also, the news media may catch a political candidate in a lie, but unions and employers do not have reporters checking on their statements. In 1962, the Board's rule was that a new election would be held if the winner lied about an important fact shortly before the election. In 1977, the Board repealed this rule and ignored propaganda. In 1978, the Board went back to the 1962 rule, and in 1982 the Board repealed it again. Since 1982, the rule has been that false campaign propaganda is not a reason to hold a new election unless forged documents are used or the neutrality of the Board is compromised.*

Captive Audience Speeches

Another issue pertaining to organizing is whether an employer should be permitted to give a captive audience speech and, if so, whether the union should be given equal time to respond. A captive audience speech occurs when the employer assembles her employees and speaks about the union during paid working hours. The Board permits such speeches, and the employer is not required to give the union time to reply. However, to avoid emotional appeals that the other side does not have time to answer, a captive audience speech may not be given during the twenty-four hours just before an election.

Threats

The Labor Act forbids employers to threaten to punish workers if they join or vote for a union. For example, employers may not say they will cut pay or lay off workers if the union wins the election. An employer is free to close the business rather than deal with a union, but (except in the rarest of cases) an employer may not threaten workers that the business will be closed if they choose to unionize. An employer may make a prediction about the future if the prediction is based on fact. So an employer may say workers could be laid off if the union wins the election and successfully negotiates for a fifty-cent raise—provided the employer has evidence that a fifty-cent raise would lead to layoffs.

Similarly, the Act forbids unions from threatening to punish workers if they do not join or vote for the union. For example, a union may not tell workers that they do not have to pay initiation fees if they join the union before the election, but they will have to pay initiation fees if they join afterwards. The reason is that workers will feel threatened that they will be penalized (by having to pay initiation fees) if they do not join before the election. But a union may offer to waive initiation fees if the offer remains open after the election.

* See below in this chapter REMEDIES FOR IRREGULARITIES, Rerun Elections.

Promises

The law forbids employers from making promises to workers if they reject the union. Thus, an employer may not promise to raise pay if the union loses the election. (In fact, an employer may not actually raise pay shortly before an election if workers would perceive the raise as an implied promise or threat.) Unions are also forbidden from making promises to workers during organizing. Union promises are not a serious problem, though, because it is assumed that the union does not have the power by itself to keep them. Thus, when a union says it will get a fifty-cent raise, the workers understand that the union cannot raise their pay without the employer's agreement.

Polls

The final issue about organizing to be considered is whether employers and unions may question workers concerning their feelings toward unionization. During an organizing campaign, both sides have a great desire to know where the workers stand; yet interrogation can be intimidating. The law distinguishes between systematic polls to find out what all the workers think and occasional discussions with individual workers.

Systematic Polls   An employer usually has no legitimate reason to question workers about their feelings toward a union, and such questioning is often intimidating. As a result, the general rule is that an employer may not poll workers to find out how they feel about unionizing. There is, however, one exception. A union may claim to represent the majority of workers in a bargaining unit and, on this basis, the union may ask the employer to recognize it without an election. The employer may honor the union's claim—that is, recognize and bargain with the union—only if it is truly the majority representative; therefore, before deciding to recognize the union, the employer has a good reason to find out how the workers feel about the union. But the risk of intimidating the workers still exists. To protect against intimidation, the employer must tell them why she is asking about their opinions of the union, and must assure the workers that she will not punish them for expressing their opinions; also, the poll must be conducted by secret ballot, and the employer must not be guilty of any other unfair labor practices.

Occasional Discussions   Occasional, isolated discussions with workers are treated differently. The typical case is a conversation between a supervisor (for example, a foreman) and a worker in which the topic of the union comes up. Is the employer (through her agent) intimidating the worker, or is it merely a casual discussion of a topic of mutual concern? The Board decides by taking into account all the surrounding circumstances. For example, a question from a foreman may be less intimidating than a question from the vice president for personnel. The location of the conversation is important: a talk on the floor of the shop, with other workers nearby, may be less intimidating than an individual interview in a supervisor's office. The status of the worker is relevant: an open supporter of the union is less likely to be intimidated than an uncommitted worker. Other circumstances may be important as well, such as whether the supervisor or the worker raised the topic and whether the employer has committed separate unfair labor practices.

No rule prohibits a union from polling workers about their opinions of it. The reason is that a union, during an organizing campaign, has little power to intimidate workers. As noted above, however, a union does have the power to threaten workers. Therefore, if a representative of a union asks a worker whether she supports it, and makes her feel that the union will take revenge against her if she says no, the questioning is illegal.

ELECTIONS

As discussed in chapter 3,* there are two common kinds of election, certification and decertification, and they are usually held for one of three purposes: (1) workers who are not currently represented by a union vote on whether they want the union to become their bargaining agent; (2) workers who already have a union vote on whether to replace it with another union; and (3) workers who have a union vote on whether to oust it and return to individual bargaining with the employer. Two issues concerning elections are when they may be held (that is, the timing of elections) and who may vote (that is, the eligibility of voters).

* Chapter 3, REPRESENTATION CASES, Certification Cases and Decertification Cases.

Timing of Elections

The basic rule is that an election may be held at any time when at least 30 percent of the workers wants to vote on whether to certify or decertify a union. However, there are so many exceptions to the basic rule, and they are so large, that it can truly be said that the exceptions have swallowed the rule.

One exception is that no election may be held until at least twelve months after a preceding election. The purpose of this rule is to avoid the turmoil of frequent elections. (The twelve-month rule does not apply to a rerun election. If the Board voids an election—for example, because of serious misconduct—a rerun election can be held at once.)

Another exception is that the Board will not allow an election for a reasonable time (usually, one year) after a union becomes the bargaining agent for a unit. The reason is to give the union time to establish itself with the workers and the employer.

A third exception to the basic rule is that, except for a brief "window period" near the expiration of the contract, the Board will not hold an election during the first three years of the term of a collective bargaining contract. (If the contract lasts less than three years, the rule applies until the contract expires. If the contract lasts more than three years, the rule applies until the end of the third year.) This exception is known as the contract bar (the contract is a bar to an election), and it exists because of the high value the Board places on stability in labor relations. But stability competes with another value, namely, the interest of workers in being represented by the union of their choice or by no union at all. The workers' interest is the reason that the contract bar applies only during the first three years of a contract; it would be unfair to workers if an employer and a union could sign a long contract and cut off the workers' right to an election for many years.

Two footnotes and a proviso to the contract bar are important. The first footnote is that the law does not forbid long labor contracts. An employer and union are legally free to write an agreement that will last for four or five years or even longer. Nonetheless, the contract bar lasts only during the initial three years of the agreement.

The second footnote is that the contract bar expires with the contract. If there is no labor agreement in effect (and if none of the exceptions discussed above applies), an election may be held at any time.

The proviso to the contract bar is that the Board will accept a petition for an election that is filed during the "window period" of sixty to ninety days before the end of a labor agreement. (The window closes during the final sixty days of a contract because negotiations are usually intense during this period and would be disrupted by an election.) It is common for a new agreement to take effect immediately after the old one expires. In many cases, therefore, the only opportunity for workers to ask for an election to change unions or to get rid of their union is during the window that opens on the ninetieth day and closes on the sixtieth day (that is, during the third-to-the-last month) preceding the expiration of a labor agreement.

Eligibility to Vote in General

Whenever the Labor Board conducts an election of any kind, it must be decided who is eligible to vote. Naturally, all full-time workers on the job in the bargaining unit are eligible. But what about workers on part-time schedules, on layoff, or on strike? The basic rule is that employees may vote if they have a reasonable expectation of continued employment or reemployment. If Mary has worked twenty-five hours a week for several years, she is a permanent part-time employee and would be allowed to vote. If Harry has been on layoff for six months and stands last on the recall list, and production is about to be cut back again, he has little hope of reemployment and would not be allowed to vote.

An interesting question is whether a "salt" should be allowed to vote in an election. When a union seeks to organize a shop, one of the union's paid organizers sometimes takes a job in the shop in order to have easy access to the workers. This practice is called "salting," and the organizer is a "salt." If the organization drive is successful enough for the union to petition the Board to hold an election, the salt wants to vote. Knowing how the salt will vote, the employer does not want the salt to vote. Two issues arise. First, is the salt an employee of the company? Employers argue that the salt is an employee of the union, not of the company, and should not be allowed to vote. Unions argue that a worker may be an employee of two different employers at the same time, for example, a worker who holds a day and an evening job. Employers respond that a salt takes orders from, and is loyal to, the union, not the company. Unions reply that a salt has to follow the company's orders during working hours like any other worker. The Board has held that a salt is an employee of the company and may vote in the election, and the courts have agreed. Therefore, it would be an unfair labor practice for an employer to refuse to hire or to discharge someone suspected of being a salt. The second issue is whether a salt should be allowed to vote in a representation election. If a salt does not have enough in common with the other workers, the salt should not be allowed to vote on whether or not they will unionize. Employers argue that a salt will quit the job immediately after the election, does not depend on this job for a living, and, therefore, has little in common with the other workers in the unit. Unions argue that the same may be true of other workers, who may, or may not, depend on this job for a living and, in any event, are free to quit a job whenever they please. The Board usually allows salts to vote.

Eligibility to Vote during Strikes

Strikes create new categories of employee under the Labor Act, and each category has its own voting rights. It is important to define these categories before exploring the rights attached to them.

There are two categories of strikers. An unfair labor practice striker is protesting the employer's illegal behavior, such as refusing to bargain in good faith or interfering with concerted activity. A worker on strike for any other legal reason—for example, in protest of the employer's wages or working conditions—is an economic striker. It is important to remember that, under the Labor Act, both categories of strikers remain employees during a strike.

The Labor Act allows employers to hire replacements for strikers. Replacements are employees under the Act. There are two categories of replacements. A temporary replacement is hired only for the length of the strike and expects to be discharged when the strike is over. A permanent replacement is hired for an indefinite period and expects to be kept on the job even after the strike is settled.

The eligibility of an employee to vote during a strike depends on these factors: whether it is an unfair labor practice strike or an economic strike and whether replacement workers are temporary or permanent. But before discussing the specific rules on eligibility to vote during strikes, the practical significance of these rules should be explained. The purpose of an election held during a strike is usually to decertify the union. Strikers will probably vote in favor of the union; replacements will probably vote against it. Accordingly, employers, who generally want to get rid of unions, want replacements to be allowed to vote and strikers to be prohibited from voting. Unions, of course, want just the opposite. The rules on eligibility of voters, therefore, will probably have a direct effect on the outcome of the elections held during strikes.

Economic Strikes   As noted above, the basic rule is that an employee may vote if she has a reasonable expectation of employment or reemployment. This rule holds during economic strikes, in which the strikers are protesting wages and working conditions, and the rule applies to replacements and to strikers alike. Let us now apply this rule to specific cases.

A permanent replacement expects to keep her job after the strike is settled; accordingly, she may vote. A temporary replacement expects to be discharged when the strikers return to work; she may not vote.

An economic striker who has not been replaced expects to return to his job; he may vote. An economic striker who has been temporarily replaced also expects to return to work and may vote. An economic striker whose job has been eliminated (for example, because the employer has reorganized production during the strike) has little hope of returning to work, so she may not vote. The same is true for an economic striker who abandons the strike and finds another permanent job.

The hardest case is the economic striker who has been permanently replaced. This worker still wants his job. The permanent replacement might keep the job for a month or a decade. Up until 1947, an economic striker who had been permanently replaced was permitted to vote. From 1947 to 1959, he was not permitted to vote. Then a compromise was struck. Since 1959, an economic striker who has been permanently replaced may vote during the first year of the strike, but not afterward. (The rules above still apply. If the striker's job has been eliminated or he has abandoned the strike and accepted a permanent job elsewhere, he may not vote.)

Unfair Labor Practice Strikes   During unfair labor practice strikes, in which the strikers are protesting behavior of their employer that violates the Labor Act, the strikers may be temporarily—but not permanently—replaced. Therefore, a replacement will not keep her job, and she may not vote. Similarly, the striker expects to return to her job, and she may vote. The one-year rule does not apply to unfair labor practice strikers. A worker on an unfair labor practice strike may vote whenever the election is held, regardless of how long the strike has lasted (assuming her job still exists and she has not abandoned the strike and accepted permanent work with another firm).

REMEDIES FOR IRREGULARITIES

Rerun Elections

The Labor Board has power to order an election to be rerun if irregularities occur that may have affected the outcome of the election. Sometimes, the irregularity amounts to an unfair labor practice. For example, if a union officer threatens to blacklist any worker who votes against the union (that is, prevent the worker from getting a job), or the employer threatens to fire any worker who votes for the union, a rerun election would be in order.

Other times, the irregularity is not an unfair labor practice; nevertheless, the Board concludes that the voters' right to a free choice was compromised, and a rerun election is called. Thus, telling lies about the other side during an election campaign is not an unfair labor practice, but, as mentioned above, during some periods of its history the Board has considered false propaganda to be an irregularity that justified a new election. Another example of an irregularity that would justify a new election, without being an unfair labor practice, is an attempt by an employer or a union to convince the workers that the Board or the federal government wants them to vote one way or the other; a common technique is the distribution of copies of an official ballot with a box already marked.

Bargaining Orders

It was mentioned above that the Labor Board must order a respondent who has committed an unfair labor practice to cease and desist, and the Board may order the respondent to make victims whole for their losses. Thus, if an employer prohibits workers from soliciting for a union on company property during nonworking time, and fires a worker who solicits during the lunch break, the Board will order the employer to rescind the prohibition and reinstate the worker with back pay and seniority.

An additional remedy may be necessary for especially serious unfair labor practices that occur during organizing. This remedy, known as a bargaining order, is appropriate when an employer's unfair labor practices are so numerous and so serious that a fair election (either initial or rerun) is impossible; that is, even if the employer stopped the illegal behavior, made victims whole for their losses, and notified the workers of these steps, the effect of the unfair labor practices could not be erased from the voters' minds. In this event, the Board has power to order the employer to recognize and bargain with the union.

The theory behind a bargaining order is that most of the workers once supported the union, but the employer's illegal conduct has so intimidated them that they are afraid to continue their support. Therefore, the Board will issue a bargaining order only if the union can demonstrate that it enjoyed majority support at some time in the past.

5

THE DUTY
TO BARGAIN

The purpose of the Labor Act is to promote collective bargaining. Collective bargaining is defined as the duty "to meet at reasonable times and confer in good faith with respect to wages, hours, and other terms and conditions of employment." Sections 8(a)(5) and 8(b)(3) make it an unfair labor practice for an employer or a union to refuse to observe the duty to bargain. This chapter deals with how the duty to bargain is applied to specific situations.

"TO MEET . . . AND CONFER"

If neither side wishes to discuss anything, there is no duty to meet. One side must request a meeting. Such a request is rarely refused, but attempts to delay the meeting are not uncommon. Unreasonable delays can add up to a refusal to bargain and are against the law.

Another kind of refusal to bargain occurs if one side requests a meeting, and the other side imposes unreasonable conditions. For example, it is illegal for an employer to agree to meet only on the condition that the union call off a strike; it is illegal for a union to submit a proposal only on the condition that the employer accept or reject it the same day. Generally, neither side may impose the condition that the other side change the members of its bargaining team.

A vexatious issue has been whether either side may insist on recording bargaining sessions. Would a word-for-word transcript make it easier to interpret the contract in the future, or would a transcript make the bargainers reluctant to speak their minds on the record? The Board holds that one party may ask the other party for permission to make a transcript, but, if the other side refuses, the subject must be dropped. (In other words, recording bargaining sessions is a permissible subject of bargaining. Permissible subjects will be discussed in more detail later in this chapter.*)

The examples of conditions so far have involved imposing conditions *prior to* the start of negotiations. Imposing unreasonable conditions *during* negotiations is also illegal. For example, a party may not insist that a particular issue be resolved before other issues are discussed. Thus, a union may not refuse to discuss seniority until safety concerns are settled; an employer may not refuse to discuss economic issues (such as wages) until all noneconomic issues (such as grievance procedures) are agreed to. If the parties cannot agree on an issue—no matter how important it is, and even if no contract is possible unless this issue is settled—they should move on to other issues and return to the troubling one later.

Information is essential to bargaining, and the parties often request information from each other. As a rule, information must be supplied as long as it is relevant to collective bargaining. A union is entitled to receive facts on the job classifications, wage rates, and fringe benefits of members of the bargaining unit. But the employer's legitimate interests may limit the union's right to information. Thus, the union might ask for a statement of the firm's profits in recent years. Based on his interest in privacy, the employer may decline to supply this information. (However, if the employer has himself raised the issue of profits by claiming he cannot afford to meet the union's demands, the union may require him to open his books.) If the reason for requesting information is improper, it may be withheld, for example, if one side wants the information in order to harass or embarrass the other publicly.

The duty to supply information applies not only during negotiations toward a new contract, but also during the term of a contract. (Indeed, the Labor Board and the courts define collective bargaining to include both bargaining for new contracts and administering existing contracts.) Accordingly, if a union needs information to process a grievance, the employer must generally supply the information.

It is a refusal to bargain for one party (usually the employer) to change the terms of employment without bargaining with the other party. Such a change is called "unilateral action" or a "unilateral change." The rule against unilateral action holds true whether or not a collective agreement is in force. When an agreement exists, of course, both parties must honor its terms. Unilateral action that changes the terms of the agreement is a

---

* See "WITH RESPECT TO WAGES, HOURS, AND OTHER TERMS AND CONDITIONS OF EMPLOYMENT," Permissible Subjects of Bargaining.

refusal to bargain. Therefore, if either side proposes a change in a labor contract during its term and the other side refuses to consent, the change may not be made.

The rules are somewhat different if no agreement is in force. The duty to bargain still applies; unilateral action is still illegal. But there are two separate situations that receive different treatment. In the first situation, the old contract has expired, and the parties are making progress toward a new one. If the employer proposes a change, and the union rejects it, the employer may not make the change. Making and rejecting proposals is what bargaining is all about; as long as the negotiations are moving along, the employer may not change the conditions of employment.

In the second situation, the old contract has expired, but the parties are not making progress toward a new one; in other words, they have reached an impasse, and negotiations have broken down. There is no longer a duty to meet and confer after an impasse; further bargaining would be fruitless. In this case, the employer may make changes that previously have been offered to the union. The reason is that an impasse can last a long time, and an employer should not be prevented from managing the business. Thus, if the employer offered a fifty-cent raise before the impasse, she may raise pay by fifty cents without the union's consent after the impasse.

It is important to realize that an impasse can be broken. One side or the other might soften its position, and further bargaining would be useful. If an impasse is broken (for example, the union reduces its wage demand by several cents), the duty to meet and confer applies once again. In this event, a unilateral change would be illegal.

As usual, there is an exception to the rule. Suppose an unorganized firm (that is, a firm that is not unionized) has regularly taken a certain action, for example, paid a bonus at the end of the year. The workers vote for a union in October, and negotiations are in progress at the end of the year. Two questions arise: First, may the employer continue to give the bonus without the union's agreement? The answer is yes: an employer may continue to follow an established program. Second, may the employer stop giving the bonus without the union's agreement? The answer is no: an employer may not abandon an established program without bargaining.

Duration of the Duty to Meet and Confer

As noted, the duty to meet and confer ceases if an impasse is reached and revives if the impasse is broken. The Labor Act specifically addresses another aspect of the duration of the duty: neither party need agree to, or even discuss, a change concerning a mandatory subject of bargaining that is contained in a contract for a fixed period of time. (A mandatory subject of bargaining is a topic that must be discussed if either side raises it. Mandatory subjects will be considered in more detail later in this chapter.*) Thus, suppose a two-year contract states that workers must produce a minimum of ten chattels per hour. When profits fall because of competition, the employer wants to raise the minimum to twelve per hour. The union may refuse to discuss the issue because it is covered by the contract. If the union does discuss the issue, the union need not agree to the employer's proposal. And, of course, it would be a unilateral change if the employer raised the minimum without the union's consent.

The rules in the preceding paragraph dealt with a mandatory subject of bargaining that is contained in a contract. Not every mandatory subject can be contained in every labor contract. Suppose a mandatory subject is not discussed during negotiations and is not mentioned in the contract. Is there a duty to bargain over such a subject during the term of the contract? The answer is yes. Thus, consider a one-year contract that runs from January 1 through December 31. The subject of pensions did not arise during bargaining, and the contract contains no clause on pensions. The union may demand bargaining on pensions on January 2 or August 15 or any other day during the year. Of course, the employer has no duty to agree to the union's proposal. Also, many contracts contain a zipper clause, which states that the parties give up the right to demand bargaining on new topics during the term of the agreement.

The duty to bargain lasts only as long as the union represents the majority of workers in a unit. An employer should not bargain with a union if the workers no longer want the union to represent them. But workers' ideas can change from day to day. If the duty to bargain existed on days when the workers were satisfied with the union, and disappeared on days when the workers were dissatisfied, the workplace would become unstable. Therefore, the law makes three assumptions. The first is that the union remains the majority's choice for a period of time after the union begins to represent a unit. (If the union has won an election and been certified by the Board, the period is one year. If the union was directly recognized by the employer without an election, the period is a reasonable

---

* See ". . . WITH RESPECT TO WAGES, HOURS, AND OTHER TERMS AND CONDITIONS OF EMPLOYMENT," Mandatory Subjects of Bargaining.

time.) The union needs time to establish itself. This assumption is so strong that it cannot be overcome by any amount of evidence. Even if all the workers freely sign a petition to get rid of the union, the employer must continue to bargain with it during the first year.*

The second assumption the law makes is that a union remains the majority's choice during the term of a collective bargaining agreement. This assumption is also very strong; for practical purposes, an employer who has signed a contract with a union must continue to deal with the union as long as the contract is in force.[†]

The third assumption is that the union remains the majority's choice at all other times. This assumption is not so strong as the others. After the union's first year, and if no contract is in effect, the employer may refuse to bargain with the union if the employer reasonably doubts that the majority still wants to be represented by the union. This doubt must be based on objective evidence and must be held in good faith. Statements by a few workers to supervisors that the workers are unhappy with the union would not be enough evidence for an employer to cease bargaining with a union. However, statements by most workers that they no longer want the union would be enough proof. Normal turnover in a bargaining unit (that is, an average number of new workers replacing those who have left the firm) is usually not proof that the majority no longer wants the union; the Board presumes that incoming workers favor the union in the same proportion as outgoing workers did. In contrast, exceptionally high turnover in a short period of time might, if coupled with evidence of the workers' dissatisfaction with the union, indicate that the union has lost the majority's support.

" . . . IN GOOD FAITH . . ."

The duty to bargain requires that the parties negotiate in good faith. It is not enough that they meet and say no to each other; they must genuinely try to reach agreement.

---

* Another aspect of this rule was mentioned in chapter 4: the Labor Board will not accept a petition for an election to decertify a union during its first year as representative. See chapter 4, ELECTIONS, Timing of Elections.
† Again, an aspect of this rule was noted in chapter 4: under the contract bar rule, the Board will not accept a petition to decertify a union while a contract is in effect, except during the third-to-last month of the contract. See chapter 4, ELECTIONS, Timing of Elections.

Good faith is a state of mind. Determining what is going on in someone else's mind is never easy. We can ask the person, of course, but if his guilt or innocence is at stake, we are not likely to take his word about what he was thinking. As a result, we must rely on external evidence to reveal the person's internal state of mind.

Perhaps the most tempting evidence of whether a party is bargaining in good faith is how much he concedes to the other side during bargaining. Someone who is unwilling to reach agreement will probably refuse to make concessions. Yet such reasoning carries the great danger that the government might end up writing contracts for employers and unions: for if the Labor Board could decide whether a concession is large enough (good-faith bargaining) or too small (bad-faith bargaining), the government would have a powerful influence over collective bargaining. To avoid this danger, the Labor Act specifically states that the duty to bargain does not require either party to agree to a proposal or make a concession. Nevertheless, the Board considers that failure to make a concession can be evidence of bad faith. Failure to concede *plus* other evidence may establish a refusal to bargain.

A party who rejects every proposal from the other side and gives no reasons—and so makes bargaining impossible—has refused to bargain in good faith. So too have a party who makes only proposals that she knows the other side cannot accept and a party who locks herself into a position that prevents her from accepting offers from the other side. A final example: an employer who insists on terms that would leave the workers no better off than they would be without the union could be on the wrong side of the law. This last example may be troubling. Should not a strong employer be allowed to get maximum concessions from a weak union? It can be difficult to distinguish a fair-minded employer who wants the best deal possible from a closed-minded employer who wants to destroy the union.

"... WITH RESPECT TO WAGES, HOURS, AND OTHER TERMS AND CONDITIONS OF EMPLOYMENT"

If a union wants to negotiate over how the profits of the business will be spent, does the employer have a duty to bargain about this topic, and may the union call a strike if the employer does not accept the union's proposal? If an employer wants to negotiate over which candidate for

Congress the union will support in the next election, does the union have a duty to bargain about this topic, and may the employer lock out the workers if the union will not accept his proposal? In general, which subjects must employers and unions bargain over, and may they use economic force to obtain agreement about these subjects?

Mandatory Subjects of Bargaining

As noted in the first paragraph of this chapter, the Labor Act defines the duty to bargain as the obligation to meet and confer over "wages, hours, and other terms and conditions of employment." According to the Labor Board and the courts, this definition shows that Congress intended the duty to bargain to apply to topics that directly affect the employment relationship. Wages directly affect the employment relationship. If a union wants to discuss wages, the employer must bargain in good faith about them. Seniority directly affects the employment relationship. If an employer wants to discuss seniority, the union must bargain in good faith about it. These topics are called "mandatory subjects of bargaining." Each party may use economic weapons—such as strikes and lockouts— to force the other party to agree to a proposal on a mandatory subject.

Permissible Subjects of Bargaining

Congress also intended that the duty to bargain should not apply to topics that do not directly affect the employment relationship. Collective bargaining is permitted over such topics, but it is not required. A firm's advertising policy does not directly affect the employment relationship. If the union wants to discuss advertising policy, the employer is free to negotiate—or to refuse to negotiate. How the union decides whether to go on strike does not directly affect the employment relationship. If the employer wants to discuss strike votes, the union is likewise free to negotiate—or to refuse to negotiate. These topics are called "permissible subjects of bargaining." Economic weapons may *not* be used to force agreement to a proposal on a permissible subject.

Illegal Subjects of Bargaining

There is a third category of topics, called "illegal subjects of bargaining." As its name implies, this category includes topics that may not lawfully be included in a labor contract—for example, a closed shop clause or a racially discriminatory clause. The duty to bargain is violated if such topics are even proposed to the other side; and, of course, economic force may not be used to secure an agreement on an illegal subject.

Distinguishing Mandatory from Permissible Subjects

It is relatively easy to know which topics are illegal: one law or another forbids them. But how can one know which topics are mandatory and which are permissible? As stated above, the standard is whether the subject directly affects the employment relationship. This standard is vague, however, and people can disagree about it. For example, suppose a union wants to bargain about the firm's investment policy; perhaps the union thinks the company should invest in new equipment for the plant instead of letting it run down. Does investment policy directly affect the employment relationship? Yes, argues the union. If the equipment is not updated, the plant will eventually become unprofitable; it will be closed, and the workers will lose their jobs. The employment relationship is directly affected because there will be no employment relationship if the plant closes. No, argues the employer. How to use capital is a decision for management to make. Workers may be *indirectly* affected, but investment decisions are far removed from the employment relationship.

The arguments on both sides seem strong. How can one know which side the law will favor? Most issues that concern workers have probably come up in the past. If so, there is a precedent on record; that is, the Labor Board or the courts have already decided whether the subject is mandatory or permissible, and that decision will be honored in the future. There are long lists of subjects that have been held to be mandatory or permissible. If a particular topic is on the lists, legal research can provide a definite answer. Here follow a few examples of mandatory subjects:

- rate of pay (that is, how much?);
- method of pay (salary, hourly, piece rate, commission);
- hours of work;
- work rules;
- safety;
- promotions;
- health insurance;
- pensions;
- order of layoffs;

- benefits for workers who are laid off;
- discipline;
- drug testing;
- grievance and arbitration procedures;
- effects of a major change in operations (such as closing a plant).

Any topic that is not mandatory or illegal is permissible. Here follow a few examples of permissible subjects:

- change in the bargaining unit;
- identity of the bargaining agent;
- internal union affairs;
- status of supervisors;
- settlement of unfair labor practice charges;
- union representation on the board of directors;
- decision to make a major change in operations (such as closing a plant).

In the example of investment policy, the law agrees with the employer. Investment policy is a permissible, but not a mandatory, subject of bargaining.

Sometimes, however, an issue has not come up before. In this event, the new issue will be compared to those already on the lists. Is it like topic A, which has been held to be mandatory, or more like topic Z, which has been held to be permissible? Legal research cannot give a definite answer; only the Board and courts can.

A final word about mandatory subjects is in order. It was said at the beginning of this chapter that, if neither side wishes to discuss anything, there is no duty to meet.* The same principle applies to mandatory subjects. If neither side raises a mandatory subject during bargaining, the agreement will simply be silent on the point. In other words, not every mandatory subject has to be included in every labor contract. But if one side chooses to raise a mandatory subject, both sides must bargain about it in good faith.

REMEDIES FOR A REFUSAL TO BARGAIN

The remedy for an unfair labor practice is an order to cease and desist from the illegal conduct.† Also, if an individual loses wages or seniority, the Board usually orders the guilty respondent to make up for those losses.

---

* See "TO MEET AND CONFER"
† See chapter 2, SECTION 8: UNFAIR LABOR PRACTICES, Remedies for Unfair Labor Practices.

The remedies for a refusal to bargain are parallel. The guilty party is always ordered to cease violating the law, in other words, to bargain in good faith in the future. If specific losses can be proved, the Board may order them to be made up. For example, if an employer unilaterally cuts wages from eight dollars an hour to seven, the Board may order the employer to pay the eight-dollar rate in the future (at least until bargaining can occur) and to pay the workers one dollar for each hour they worked at the seven-dollar rate.

Another common example—and a more difficult one to deal with—is the employer who violates the law by refusing to bargain in good faith during negotiations. The topic is often wages. What should the remedy be for this violation? A cease-and-desist order is appropriate, of course, but what about money? Both employers and unions agree that the workers lose, and the guilty employer saves, the *difference* between the wages that would have been agreed to during good faith bargaining *and* the wages that actually were paid. For example, if good-faith bargaining would have led to wages of twelve dollars an hour, while the employer was paying only eleven dollars and fifty cents, the workers have lost fifty cents an hour.

But now the parties disagree. Unions argue that the employer refuses to bargain in good faith purposely to save money. The workers would have received this money if the employer had obeyed the law. Therefore, say unions, the Board should order the employer to pay the illegal savings to the workers. Employers reply that there is no way to know how much the employer saved; we do not know what the outcome of good-faith bargaining would have been. We can only guess that good-faith bargaining would have led to wages of twelve dollars an hour. Also, if the Board starts saying what the outcome of good faith bargaining would be, the government will end up writing contracts for the parties.

The Board accepts the employers' arguments. The remedy for refusing to bargain over wages is an order to bargain over wages in the future. As a result, unions must rely on their economic power to get increased wages.

6

ECONOMIC WEAPONS

If collective bargaining is unsuccessful, employers and unions may resort to economic force to get what they want. This chapter discusses the rules of economic warfare.

EMPLOYERS' ECONOMIC WEAPONS

Right to Refuse to Accept Union Demands

An employer's most powerful economic weapon is the right to refuse to agree to a union's demands. When a union asks for more money or better working conditions, and an employer says no, the law allows the business to stay open and the terms of employment to remain the same. The union must then accept the present terms or attempt to force the employer to change.

Right to Replace Economic Strikers

An employer's second most powerful economic weapon is the legal right to replace economic strikers. Thus, if a union strikes for higher pay, a health insurance plan, and so on, the employer may hire replacements and keep the business operating. Further, the law permits the employer to treat the replacements as either temporary or permanent employees. If the employer hires temporary replacements, the strikers can expect to get their jobs back when the strike is over. If the employer hires permanent replacements, however, the strikers have lost their jobs for practical purposes; even if the strikers offer to return to work, the employer is free to keep the permanent replacements on the job.

A striker who abandons the strike, crosses the picket line, and returns to work, is called a "cross-over." An employer may treat a cross-over like a permanent replacement worker. Thus, if a cross-over takes a job that used to be held by a striker, the employer may declare that the striker has been permanently replaced.

Economic strikers—whether or not they have been replaced—remain employees in the eyes of the law. As a result, when a permanent replacement leaves a job (quits or is fired), the striker who used to hold that job (and who has applied for reinstatement) has a right of recall; and the employer must notify the striker that the job is available. The striker loses the right of recall, however, if his old job is abolished and he is not qualified for other jobs, or if he abandons the strike and accepts a permanent job with another firm.

No Right to Replace Unfair Labor Practice Strikers

Strikers who are protesting an unfair labor practice are treated differently from economic strikers.* The employer may hire temporary—but not permanent—replacements if the strike is caused by an unfair labor practice, for example, the employer's refusal to bargain in good faith. If unfair labor practice strikers offer to return to work, the employer must accept them and discharge the replacements.

There are two risks for unfair labor practice strikers. The first is that they can be mistaken about the illegality of their employer's action; if the Board holds that the employer did not commit an unfair labor practice, the strikers will be treated like economic strikers (so that the employer could permanently replace them). The second risk is that the Board might not believe that the reason for the strike was the employer's unfair labor practice. Regardless of what the strikers feel, if the Board believes the strike was really caused by economic issues—for example, the Board thinks the strike was not caused by the employer's failure to bargain in good faith, but by the workers' desire for higher wages—the strikers will be treated like economic strikers.

Unfair labor practice strikes also pose a risk for employers. If an unfair labor practice striker offers to return to work (and the striker's job still exists; for example, it is held by a replacement worker), the employer must reinstate the striker. If the employer refuses, the striker is entitled to back pay from the date of refusal. But like a striker, an employer cannot

---

* See chapter 4, ELECTIONS, Eligibility to Vote during Strikes.

be certain how the Board will classify the strike. If the Board decides it is an economic strike, the employer has no duty to reinstate the striker; but if the Board decides it is an unfair labor practice strike, the employer must reinstate the striker or be liable for back pay.

Right to Lock Out

Another powerful economic weapon an employer may use is the lockout. Lockouts over mandatory subjects of bargaining are legal. Thus, an employer may lock out to force the union to agree to her terms of employment, even though the workers are content to accept present conditions and continue bargaining. As long as the employer is motivated by a good reason (and putting pressure on the union is considered a good reason), a lockout is legal. But if a lockout is motivated by a bad reason, the lockout is illegal. An employer may not lock out to frighten workers into voting against the union in an upcoming election or to convince them that collective bargaining is useless and they should abandon their union; nor may an employer lock out to obtain agreement on a permissible subject of bargaining.

May an employer who has lawfully locked out her workers then hire replacements? It is settled that this employer may hire temporary replacements. At this writing, there are no cases on whether this employer may hire permanent replacements.

UNIONS' ECONOMIC WEAPONS

Most strikes are concerted activity, and the strikers are protected by the Labor Act. An employer may not discriminate against workers because they have participated in a strike. Thus, if a striker offers to return to work, the employer must put him back on the job—provided several conditions are satisfied: First, the job still exists; that is, the employer has not reorganized work and abolished the job. Second, business conditions require the job to be filled; if production has been reduced (whether because of the strike or other causes), the striker may be laid off. Third, a permanent replacement has not taken the job. Fourth, the striker has not been discharged for misconduct during the strike (for example, abusing customers who crossed the picket line). Fifth, the striker has not abandoned the strike and accepted permanent work elsewhere. Also, an employer may not discriminate among strikers who offer to return to work, for example, by refusing to reinstate the leaders of the strike.

Illegal Strikes

Some strikes are not protected, however; they are often called "illegal strikes." An illegal strike does not mean the strikers can be sent to jail; rather, "illegal" here means that the strike is not protected by the Labor Act. If a strike is illegal, the employer is allowed to retaliate against the strikers, for example, by firing them. It is important, therefore, to know which kinds of strike are illegal. Several of the most common kinds are discussed here.

Many collective bargaining agreements contain a promise by the union not to strike. If the union violates this promise, the strike would be illegal. (Note, however, that the Labor Act states that quitting work because of abnormally dangerous conditions is not a strike.) There is an exception to this rule. A strike over a serious unfair labor practice is not illegal, regardless of whether there is a no-strike clause in a contract.

A strike designed to force an employer to break a law is illegal. If the government imposed a freeze on wages and a union struck for a raise, the strike would be illegal. Another example of an illegal strike is one intended to force an employer to fire a worker who broke a union rule; as discussed in chapter 2,* a union may cause an employer to fire a worker for only one reason—failure to pay dues.

A strike to force an employer to agree on a nonmandatory subject of bargaining is illegal. A union might want an employer to contribute to a fund for the promotion of the industry. This topic of bargaining is permissible (the parties may lawfully agree to such a clause), but it is not mandatory (the employer may refuse to discuss it). If the union strikes to pressure the employer to agree to contribute to the fund, the strike would be illegal.

A "wildcat strike"—that is, a strike that is not approved by the union— is almost always illegal. Suppose, for example, the union and the employer are discussing a new contract. A few workers are not satisfied with the negotiations and, without approval from the union, walk off the job. They are on a wildcat strike, and the employer is free to fire them.

---

* See chapter 2, SECTION 8: UNFAIR LABOR PRACTICES, Union Security.

A strike that creates a risk of damage to the employer's plant is illegal. In one case, workers struck without warning when molten iron could have damaged the containment vessel. They were unprotected.

Slowdowns are another kind of illegal strike. If workers could slow down on the job, rather than walk out, they would have a very effective weapon: production would fall while the workers would be drawing pay. Believing that this weapon is too powerful and that a worker should put in a day's work for a day's pay, the courts have held that slowdowns are illegal. For the same reason, refusal to work overtime is unprotected, even if the workers are protesting excessive overtime assignments (unless a labor contract allows workers to refuse overtime).

As mentioned in chapter 2,* a worker who refuses to cross a picket line is engaged in protected activity. If that picket line is part of an illegal strike, however, the worker who refuses to cross the line is out of luck: she is unprotected, just as the strikers are.

Workers participating in a legal strike can lose their protection if their behavior is improper. Strikers remain employees, and if they do something their employer would normally punish employees for, they can be disciplined. Violence is a clear example. Disrespectful language to supervisors or customers is another.

Secondary Boycotts

A strike that is part of a secondary boycott is also illegal. Some of the most complicated passages in the Labor Act define secondary boycotts. To illustrate the central idea, suppose a union has a labor dispute with an employer (called the primary employer because the dispute is primarily between her and the union). The law permits the union to put economic pressure on the primary employer—for example, a strike or a boycott of her products. But suppose the primary pressure is unsuccessful. A way for the union to increase the pressure is to use the union's power against other employers (secondary or neutral employers): for if the union can make them stop doing business with the primary employer, she will be isolated; no one will sell to her or buy from her, and she will have to give in to the union's demands. There are two principal ways for a union to force a secondary employer to stop doing business with a primary em-

* See chapter 2, SECTION 7: PROTECTION FOR CONCERTED ACTIVITY.

ployer: the union may picket or strike (or threaten to strike) the secondary employer, or the union members who are employees of the secondary employer may refuse to handle goods bought from or sold to the primary employer. These tactics are secondary boycotts. If legal, they would make unions much stronger against employers. But these tactics are considered unfair to secondary employers because they are forced to get involved in other employers' labor problems. For these reasons, secondary boycotts are illegal.

The following example illustrates these concepts:

UNION

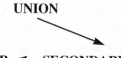

PRIMARY EMPLOYER ◄— **SECONDARY EMPLOYER**

(manufacturer)   (supplier)

Suppose a union has a dispute with a manufacturer; perhaps the manufacturer refuses to meet the union's demand for an increase in pay. The union strikes. The union also organizes a boycott, that is, asks the public not to buy the manufacturer's products. Both the strike and the boycott are primary activities because they are caused by a labor dispute and are aimed at the primary employer. The strike and boycott are not successful, so the union approaches several of the manufacturer's suppliers and requests that they stop selling raw materials to the manufacturer. The request, unaccompanied by any threat, is lawful. But one supplier refuses and continues to sell to the manufacturer. The union then pickets the supplier. This picketing is an illegal secondary boycott because the union has no labor dispute with the supplier and has used force to prevent the supplier from doing business with another employer.

In general, a union may picket the premises of a primary employer and may not picket the premises of a secondary employer. But there are three exceptions to this rule. First, a union may picket a secondary employer who is an ally of the primary employer. An ally is an employer who performs work during a strike that would normally have been performed by the strikers. For example, suppose a union strikes company A, which makes computers. Companies X and Y agree that, during the strike, they will make the computers that Company A would normally make. X and Y are allies of A, and the union may picket them.

The second exception to the rule against picketing secondary employers is the case of the "roving situs." As usual, the starting point is a labor dispute between a union and a primary employer. Consider the typical case in which the union wants higher wages, but add that the employees of the primary employer do their work on the premises of secondary employers. These primary employees are (in the union's view) underpaid wherever they are sent to work; thus, the situs—or place of the dispute—roves or moves to wherever the employees are working. For example, suppose the employees of Repair Company are technicians who repair broken office equipment. They go on strike. The union may picket Repair Company's shop, but this picketing will not accomplish much because the customers never go there. The union wants to picket the places where the work is actually done—the roving situs—in this case, the offices where the broken equipment is repaired. Thus, if Mary's Accounting, Inc. uses Repair Company to fix broken computers, it would be advantageous for the union to picket Mary's place. Of course, Mary does not want pickets in front of her doors.

The law balances the interests of the union and customers like Mary. The union may picket Mary's office only when technicians from Repair Company are physically on Mary's premises, and the picket signs must make it clear that the union's dispute is with Repair Company, not with Mary.

The third exception to the rule against picketing secondary employers is somewhat like the roving situs exception. The third exception allows a union to picket secondary employers when primary *products* are being sold on the premises. It was seen above that, if a union has a dispute with a primary employer, the union may organize a boycott of the primary employer's products. An effective way to inform the public of the boycott is to picket in front of stores that sell the products being boycotted. The stores are secondary employers because they are not involved in the labor dispute and, naturally, they oppose picketing because it can drive away customers. Once again, the law balances the interests of the union and of the secondary employers, and the outcome is similar to that for roving situses. A union may picket stores that sell boycotted products as long as the pickets urge the public only to boycott the primary employer's products; the pickets may *not* urge the public to shop at another store. Even if the pickets follow this rule, it is possible that they will be illegal if the boycotted products are a major part of the store's inventory and the store could lose much of its business.

TIMING OF STRIKES AND LOCKOUTS

The Labor Act seeks to ensure that unions and employers will negotiate with each other before resorting to strikes and lockouts. Negotiations are particularly important when a collective bargaining agreement is about to expire. Section 8(d), therefore, requires two notices before industrial warfare may begin. First, if either party wants to change or terminate a labor contract, that party must notify the other party in writing at least sixty days before the contract expires. During this sixty-day period, the union may not strike over economic issues, and the employer may not lock out. Second, if a new contract has not been settled within thirty days of the first notice, the party that wants change must notify state and federal mediation services that a labor dispute exists. (Somewhat different rules apply to health care institutions.) The penalty for striking or locking out without giving these notices or during the sixty-day period is severe: the worker who strikes prematurely loses the protection of the Labor Act. That is, for legal purposes the striker returns to the nineteenth century, and the employer is free to fire or otherwise punish the striker. The employer who locks out prematurely is obliged to pay her workers for the time they were wrongfully locked out.

7

ENFORCEMENT OF LABOR CONTRACTS

Suppose negotiations between a company and a union have been successful. An agreement has been approved, and there is peace for a while. Nevertheless, disputes are likely to arise over what the agreement means or how it should be applied to a specific case. Usually, the union complains that the employer has not lived up to his promises; and, occasionally, the employer makes the same complaint about the union. These disputes are usually resolved through arbitration.

A number of labor leaders and scholars believe that unions should not rely on arbitrators or judges to make employers obey their promises in collective bargaining agreements. These persons believe unions should rely only on their own economic power. Most labor leaders, however, are willing to go to arbitration or court to enforce employers' promises. And most employers will do the same to unions if they do not keep their promises. This chapter discusses the way unions and employers normally enforce collective bargaining agreements.

ARBITRATION

Enforcing collective bargaining contracts used to be a problem. The usual way to enforce a commercial contract is a lawsuit. If Mary believes that Harry did not keep his end of a bargain, she sues him and the judge decides who is right. For technical reasons, however, unions and employers could not take their disputes to court in the past. If the union believed that the employer had violated the contract (for example, the union thought a promotion should have been based on seniority), the union often went on strike. Strikes are hard on both employers and workers; also, strikes would have crippled the war effort during the Second World War.

As a result, another method of settling labor disputes was developed before, and widely utilized during, the war. This method was arbitration, and it worked so well that it has become the most important way for union and employers to handle their disagreements. The law does not require arbitration. It is a voluntary process that the parties agree to in the labor contract. Most contracts contain arbitration clauses.

A Typical Case

Arbitration typically begins with a grievance, which is a complaint that one party—say, the union—makes about the other party's behavior. The union files the grievance with the employer, and the two parties attempt to settle it. There may be several steps in the process as the grievance is taken to higher levels of management. If the grievance is not settled by the final step, the union must decide whether to call for arbitration. This decision is often made by one of the union's officers or by a grievance committee composed of union members. Not every unsettled grievance is taken to arbitration. The committee must think about several questions, among them: Did the employer violate the contract? If so, is there enough evidence to convince an arbitrator of the violation? And, can we afford to pay our share of the cost of arbitration?* If the answers are all yes, the employer is notified that the union demands arbitration. Then the parties choose a neutral person—known as an arbitrator, arbiter, or umpire—to decide the issue. Commonly, the parties ask the Federal Mediation and Conciliation Service (FMCS) or the American Arbitration Association (AAA or Triple A) to supply a list of qualified arbitrators, and one is chosen from the list. (Sometimes, a panel of several persons, rather than a single arbitrator, is used; such panels often contain union and employer representatives as well as neutrals.) Then a date and place for the hearing are agreed upon, and the hearing is held. Evidence is offered, and arguments are made. Finally, the arbitrator decides who is right. The arbitrator's decision is called an award.

For example, suppose there are several machines in a shop. Each machine is run by an operator and a helper. An operator retires on March 31, and his helper, Mary, wants to take over the job. The labor contract says that vacancies in the job of operator will be filled by the helper with the greatest seniority, provided this person is qualified. Mary has been a

* See chapter 2, DUTY OF FAIR REPRESENTATION.

helper for ten years, longer than anyone else, but the employer decides to promote Harry, who has been with the company for twelve years (but has been a helper for only eight years).

Mary complains to her steward, who files a grievance with the foreman. In the first step of the grievance procedure, the steward and the foreman have a meeting. The steward points out that Harry was first hired as a janitor and has been a helper for only eight years. The steward argues that "seniority" in the contract means "years as a helper," and Mary has more years as a helper. He also argues that Mary is fully able to run the machine. The foreman disagrees about the meaning of the contract; he asserts that "seniority" means "total years with the company," and Harry has been with the company longer. The foreman also argues that Mary is not qualified to run the machine.

Because the grievance is not settled at the first step, the matter moves into the second step, which is a meeting between the steward and the supervisor. The same arguments are made, with the same result. The third step is a meeting between the steward and the director of personnel, with the same outcome. Then the steward takes the case to the union's grievance committee. It agrees with him over the meaning of the term "seniority." But the committee has trouble deciding whether the union will be able to prove that Mary can run the machine; she has had some pain in her back lately. Eventually, the committee decides it has a good chance of convincing an arbitrator on this point. The committee discusses the cost of arbitration (several hundred dollars, half to be paid by the employer and half by the union) and decides the case is important enough to spend the money. The union's president then writes a letter to the company demanding arbitration. The parties write a joint letter to the Federal Mediation and Conciliation Service and receive a list of arbitrators. The president and the personnel director agree on one of the persons named on the list. (If they had been unable to agree, they might have alternated striking names until only one name was left, and that person would have become the arbitrator. Or they might have requested another list of names.) The parties write a joint letter to this person. He replies that he is available on certain dates, and a hearing is scheduled. The union offers its evidence; the company does the same. The parties decide to file written arguments with the arbitrator. A few weeks later, he decides the case and sends the parties his "opinion and award." The award states that the company should promote Mary to operator and give her back pay from April 1, the date on which she should have been promoted. The opinion explains the reasons for the award.

Unfair Labor Practice Cases

An important principle to remember is that violating a collective bargaining agreement is not automatically an unfair labor practice. Congress wanted unions and employers to resolve their own disputes (through arbitration or economic force) and did not want the government to interfere in labor relations any more than necessary. For example, collective agreements often state that the employer may discipline a worker only for just cause. If an employer fires a worker because he is a Democrat, the employer has breached the contract—but has not committed an unfair labor practice.

Sometimes, however, the labor contract and the law overlap, that is, both the contract and the law may prohibit the same behavior. For example, suppose an employer fires the union steward because she is filing too many grievances. This is not just cause, so the employer has breached the contract. Furthermore, because the steward was acting as the union representative, the employer has also discriminated against her for engaging in concerted activity. In cases of overlap, the union has a choice: go to arbitration or to the Labor Board. Sometimes the union tries to do both.

Deferral after Arbitration

If the union goes to arbitration and wins, the arbitrator will probably award complete relief. In the example above, the arbitrator could order the employer to reinstate the steward with full back pay and benefits. If the union then files an unfair labor practice charge, the Board will dismiss the charge because the victim has already received all she is entitled to.

If the union goes to arbitration and loses (or the arbitrator awards only partial relief, for example, reinstatement without back pay), the union may file an unfair labor practice charge. In this event, the Board will review the arbitration proceeding. If four standards are met, the Board will defer to arbitration, that is, the Board will dismiss the case because there already has been a fair trial before the arbitrator. Three of those standards are well settled:

- the arbitration must have been fair and regular in form (the arbitrator was not biased, the parties had a chance to offer evidence and argument, and so on);

- the parties must have agreed to accept the arbitrator's award;
- the award must not be inconsistent with the Labor Act.

The fourth standard is uncertain. For many years, it was

- the issue involved in the unfair labor practice case must have been presented to, and considered by, the arbitrator.

Recently, however, the Board has loosened this standard, so that now it is enough if

- the unfair labor practice issue and the contractual issues are "parallel," and the arbitrator has been presented with the relevant facts.

There is a major difference between the old fourth standard and the new one. Under the old standard, the Board insisted that the parties and the arbitrator be aware that they were dealing with an unfair labor practice issue and that the arbitrator decide the issue; otherwise, the Board would not defer and would decide for itself whether the unfair labor practice was committed. Under the new standard, the Board will defer if evidence of the relevant facts is presented. It is possible that the parties might not realize that an unfair labor practice was at stake; in fact, it is possible that the arbitrator might not decide whether an unfair labor practice was committed—yet, under the new standard, the Board will defer to the award.

The "burden of proof" is a legal rule that indicates which party to a case is required to prove a fact. For example, the General Counsel carries the burden of proving that an employer or a union committed an unfair labor practice. The burden of proof determines who wins when the Board cannot decide whether a fact is true or false. Thus, if the Board cannot decide whether an employer fired a worker because he was insubordinate or because he supported the union, the employer will win; the General Counsel has failed to carry the burden of proof. In the past, the Board placed the burden on the party *seeking* deferral to prove the four standards mentioned above were satisfied. In effect, the Board presumed that deferral was not appropriate until it was convinced otherwise. Recently, however, the Board has shifted the burden. The rule today is that the party *opposing* deferral must convince the Board that the four standards were *not* satisfied. For practical purposes, therefore, the Board begins with the presumption that deferral is appropriate.

Deferral before Arbitration

When a labor contract and the law overlap, a union sometimes tries to bypass arbitration and go straight to the Labor Board. In this event, however, it is very likely that the Board will send the case back to arbitration. The Board will not process the union's unfair labor practice charge if three standards are satisfied. Once again, some of the standards are settled, and one is controversial. The settled standards are

- the relationship between the union and the employer is stable;
- the employer is willing to arbitrate the grievance.

The controversial standard concerns the nature of the (alleged) illegal behavior. For a number of years, the Board would send a case to arbitration only if

- the meaning of the labor contract was central to the dispute.

In other words, a case would be sent to arbitration only if the employer and the union disagreed about how to interpret the contract. If the union was right, the employer had committed an unfair labor practice; but if the employer was right, there was no unfair labor practice. For example, if an employer announced a new work rule without bargaining with the union, the new rule would be a refusal to bargain (a unilateral change) if the contract did not allow the rule; but it would be perfectly all right if the contract did allow the rule. By contrast, if the meaning of the contract was not central to the dispute, the Board would keep the case and decide it. An example of a case that, under the old standard, would not have been sent to arbitration was a charge claiming that a worker was fired for concerted activity; such a termination would violate the just-cause clause of the contract, but the meaning of the contract would not be central to the dispute. Under the Board's new standard, however, this case will be sent to arbitration if

- it is reasonable to assume that the arbitrator's decision on the contractual issue will simultaneously settle the legal issue.

Under this standard, it is probable that all cases of overlap between the law and the labor agreement will be sent to arbitration. The courts have approved the Board's broad deferral policy.

LAWSUITS

Since the enactment of the 1947 amendments to the Labor Act, the law has permitted unions and employers to sue one another in federal court for breach of a labor contract. Perhaps the most common reason for a lawsuit is to enforce an arbitration clause. Arbitration is always a voluntary process; a court will never order someone to go to arbitration unless the person has previously agreed to it. If the parties have agreed to arbitration, several legal issues may arise.

Normally, when a contract contains an arbitration clause and one party asks for arbitration of an issue, the other agrees. A legal issue arises, however, if one of the parties refuses to go to arbitration. The one who wants arbitration (the "moving party") then has to make a motion in court for an order requiring the other one (the "responding party") to arbitrate. In court, the responding party might make two arguments: first, that the dispute is not arbitrable, that is, not covered by the arbitration clause; second, that the arbitration would be a waste of time because the moving party cannot possibly win. The first argument has a slight chance of success. If the dispute is really not arbitrable, the judge will not order arbitration. For example, if a union wanted to arbitrate over which political party the employer should contribute to, the judge would surely refuse to order arbitration because the issue is outside the collective bargaining agreement. But if the responding party's argument is doubtful, and it is not clear whether the dispute is covered by the arbitration clause, the law requires the judge to order the responding party to arbitrate. The second argument has no chance at all. The judge must not consider who he thinks will win the arbitration; that question is for the arbitrator to decide. It is apparent that judges have a strong belief that arbitration is better than lawsuits for settling labor disputes; as a result, arbitration always gets the benefit of the doubt.

Suppose a matter goes to arbitration, the arbitrator makes an award, and the loser refuses to obey it. The winner may go to court for an order enforcing the arbitrator's award. The loser might argue against enforcement of the award because it is wrong, that is, because the arbitrator made a mistake. This argument, however, is never successful; the law requires the judge to enforce the award even if she believes the arbitrator was mistaken. It is obvious why this rule is necessary: if the judge could deny enforcement of an award because the arbitrator was wrong, the judge would have to receive evidence, hear arguments, and so forth, just as the arbitrator did. There would be no reason to arbitrate if the whole process had to be repeated in court.

Nonetheless, there are reasons a judge will refuse to enforce an arbitration award. One is that the arbitrator has gone beyond the contract. For example, an arbitrator might believe something is right and order a party to do it, even though the contract does not require it. Another reason is unfairness. On rare occasions, an arbitrator is biased or refuses to admit relevant evidence. A third reason is that an award requires an act that is against public policy. For example, a contract might require an act that is illegal. The arbitrator, whose job is to enforce the contract, might require the illegal act to be performed. A judge, of course, would not enforce such an award. These reasons do not occur frequently. As a rule, a judge will enforce an arbitrator's award.

Two additional points about arbitration are important. First, if a collective agreement does *not* contain an arbitration clause, either party may sue the other in court for violation of the agreement. In fact (again assuming the agreement does not contain an arbitration clause), an individual employee may sue to protect his rights under the agreement. But, second, if the agreement *does* contain an arbitration clause, all parties, including individual employees, must take all arbitrable issues to arbitration. Courts will dismiss lawsuits over labor contracts if the issues can be arbitrated. There is one exception to this rule. We saw in chapter 2* that the duty of fair representation requires a union to investigate a worker's grievance and, if the union decides not to arbitrate the grievance, the decision must rest on good reasons. If a union refuses to arbitrate a grievance for a bad reason (for example, the union president is taking revenge on a political opponent), the worker may sue in court to protect her rights. She would have to sue and defeat both the union (by proving it breached the duty of fair representation) and the employer (by proving he violated the labor contract).

Generally, if a labor contract contains an arbitration clause, the contract also contains a no-strike clause/no-lockout clause. The union promises not to strike; the employer promises not to lock out; and disagreements will go to arbitration. The idea is that arbitration substitutes for industrial warfare. This idea is so firm in the minds of the judges that they insist on it. If the parties agree to arbitration, but leave out the no-

---

* See chapter 2, DUTY OF FAIR REPRESENTATION.

strike clause, the judges will interpret the contract as though it contained such a clause.

No-strike clauses enjoy special treatment in the courts. As discussed above, if an issue can go to arbitration, the courts will not allow a lawsuit over that issue; they will require the parties to arbitrate. There is an exception to this rule for no-strike clauses. Suppose, for example, an employer violates a contract by failing to assign overtime on the basis of seniority. The union could file a grievance and go to arbitration if necessary, but the issue is so important to the union that it calls a strike instead. The strike, of course, is also a violation of the contract, and the employer could take the union to arbitration over the strike. But the courts have given the employer an even better way to deal with the strike. Even though the Norris-LaGuardia Act prohibits federal courts from issuing injunctions in labor disputes, an employer may get an injunction against a strike that is over an arbitrable issue and that violates a no-strike clause. The courts fear that, if unions could strike, employers would become unwilling to arbitrate, and the arbitration system would collapse.

An injunction against a strike can be issued only if the dispute can go to arbitration. In the example above of the union that struck over a dispute concerning assignment of overtime, the issue of overtime is covered by the arbitration clause; so the employer can get an injunction against the strike. If the dispute *cannot* go to arbitration, an injunction against a strike cannot be issued. Suppose, for example, a shop is divided into two bargaining units, one for production workers and the other for clerks. The production workers are represented by union A, and the clerks, by union B. Union A's contract with the employer expires, and the parties negotiate a new contract that contains arbitration, no-strike, and no-lockout clauses. Then union B's contract with the employer expires. The parties negotiate, but, after a time, they reach an impasse over wages, and union B strikes. Of course, the employer cannot get an injunction against union B's strike because the contract has expired. Then union A decides to help out; it goes on a sympathy strike. The employer desires an injunction against union A's strike; after all, union A's contract is still in force, and it contains a no-strike clause. Nevertheless, the employer will be denied an injunction because the cause of the strike—namely, the impasse over wages between the employer and union B—cannot be arbitrated under the contract between the employer and union A. (It should be remembered, however, that even though the employer may not get an injunction, the employer may take union A to arbitration because the union has breached the no-strike clause in the contract; and the arbitrator may award money to the employer for profits lost due to the illegal strike.)

LIABILITY OF INDIVIDUAL WORKERS

In the *Danbury Hatters* case,* an employer won a court judgment against individual workers because they boycotted his products. The memory of this case influenced Congress to state in the Labor Act that a judgment for money against a union may be collected only from the union, *not* from its members. But suppose the employer sues the workers directly. The rule is the same: employees are not personally liable to their employer for concerted activity. Of course, if the workers violate legitimate work rules (for example, curse a supervisor), the employer may discipline them, and if they break the law (for example, destroy property), the employer may sue them personally for the damage they do. But the employer may not sue them as individuals for an illegal strike or boycott.

DISCIPLINE OF UNION OFFICERS

A union officer is like any other worker: the employer may discipline her for misconduct but may not discriminate against her for concerted activity. Thus, suppose workers go on a legal strike. The employer may replace some or all of the workers, including the union officers; but the employer may not single out the officers and replace them as punishment for leading the strike.

Now suppose some workers, including officers of the union, go on a wildcat strike (or participate in other conduct prohibited by a labor agreement). As noted, the strike is illegal, and the employer may fire all the wildcatters. May the employer fire only the union officers? May the employer fire only the leaders of the illegal strike? (These are separate questions because the leaders of the illegal strike may or may not be officers of the union.)

The argument in favor of allowing the employer to single out the officers is that they have a special duty to uphold the contract. This argument

---

* Discussed in chapter 1, ROLE OF ANTITRUST LAW.

failed in court, however. If union officers behave just like other workers, the employer may not discriminate against the officers.

As for the leaders of the illegal strike, they may be punished more harshly than the followers; therefore, the employer may fire the leaders while rehiring the other workers. If the leaders happen to be officers of the union, the result is the same; they are not privileged merely because they happen to be union officers.

Nevertheless, if the union specifically promises to control wildcat strikes, the union's officers have a duty to try to put an end to an illegal work stoppage. An official who fails to carry out this duty may be disciplined for this failure.

AFTERWORD

Labor law is incomplete. It grows every day as the Labor Board and the courts interpret and apply it. Probably every reader of this bulletin has been dissatisfied with one rule of law or another.

Two issues are being contested at this writing. One concerns permanent replacements for strikers. Under current law, an employer may hire permanent replacements for strikers.* A bill has been introduced in Congress in recent years to prohibit employers from permanently replacing economic strikers. Under the bill, employers would still be allowed to hire temporary replacements for strikers; but if a striker offered to return to work, the employer would be required to take back the striker. (The bill would not require the employer to discharge the temporary replacement, but, in most cases, the replacement would be laid off because the employer would have no job for the replacement.) Employers argue that the bill would tip the balance of power towards unions. A strike would not be a serious decision if workers could demand their jobs back as soon as being out of work became painful. As a result, workers would go on strike much more often, but the issues would not be settled. Unions argue that the bill is necessary because employers have too much economic power at the present time. Workers would not strike more frequently because they lose pay and benefits. They should not have to take the risk of losing their jobs in order to improve their working conditions.

The other issue concerns employee involvement programs. Under today's law, an employer must be careful when creating committees composed of workers and supervisors.† The committees may discuss produc-

---

* See chapter 6, EMPLOYER'S ECONOMIC WEAPONS, Right to Replace Economic Strikers.

† See chapter 2, SECTION 8: UNFAIR LABOR PRACTICES, Dominating or Assisting a Labor Union.

tion issues; but if the committees discuss the terms and conditions of employment, the employer may be violating section 8(a)(2). In recent years, Congress has considered legislation to allow employers greater latitude in creating and dealing with joint committees. Employers argue that the legislation is necessary in order to promote productivity and meet the challenge of foreign competition. Unions argue that the legislation would allow employers to trick workers into believing that they are bargaining with management when, in truth, they have no power and are not bargaining.

Because the law is still growing, it can be changed. It can be improved if citizens care enough.

INDEX